CCTV

快乐中国——学汉语

Happy China–Learning Chinese

中国中央电视台
《快乐中国——学汉语》栏目组 编

深圳篇

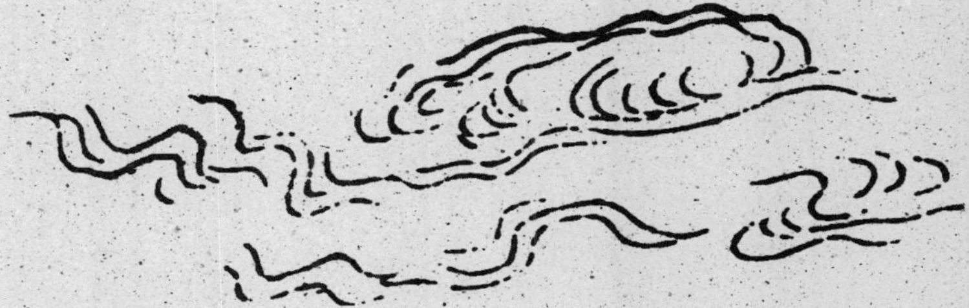

北京语言大学出版社

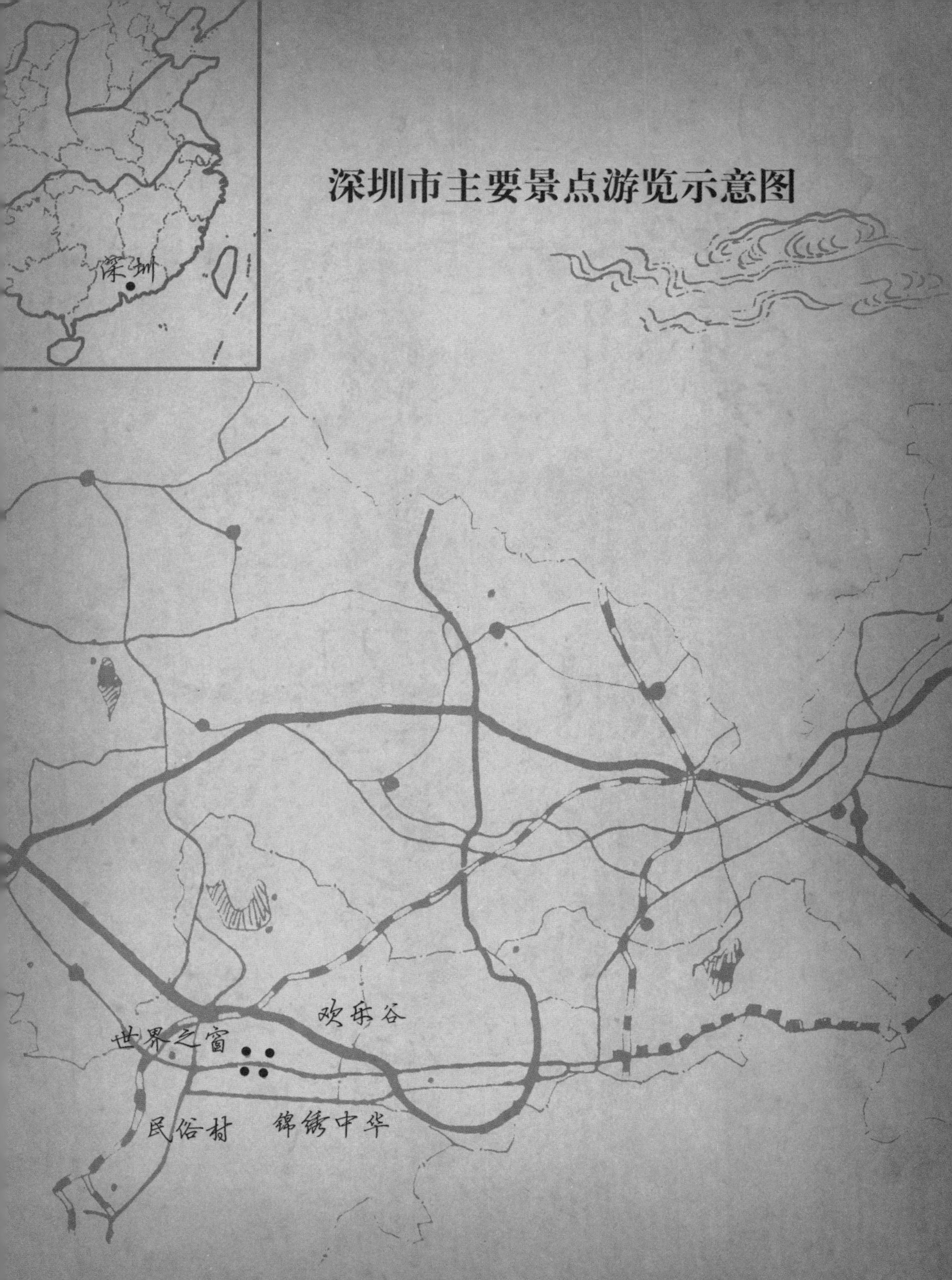
深圳市主要景点游览示意图
深圳
欢乐谷
世界之窗
民俗村
锦绣中华

前　言

中国的发展令世人瞩目，随之而来的学汉语热潮也在全球兴起。

中国中央电视台中文国际频道（CCTV-4）《快乐中国——学汉语》栏目，与中国各地城市以及风景名胜点合作，把饱览名山大川、感受中华民族历史文化与学习汉语结合起来，将汉语言语技能与知识性、趣味性和欣赏性融为一体，创办了独特的寓教于乐的电视教学节目——《快乐中国——学汉语》。

通过中央电视台覆盖全球98% 的强势传媒，《快乐中国——学汉语》自2004年6月播出以来，引起了海内外观众的热烈反响。不少观众来信来电，希望得到《快乐中国——学汉语》栏目播出节目的文字和音像材料，作为学习汉语的视听说教材。为了满足广大观众的需要，北京语言大学出版社承担了这套文字、声像教材的编辑、出版任务。在此，我们深表感谢！

语言是桥梁，电视是桥梁，《快乐中国——学汉语》是沟通你我的桥梁。它把汉语教学搬进大自然的课堂之中，“快乐学汉语，轻松又好记！”此外，我们采用高清晰电视技术和立体声制作的表现手段，并制作成可用于教学的、有多种字幕选择的DVD，充分展示汉语特有的魅力。

为了使节目主持人的对话更好地帮助您学说汉语，我们聘请了北京语言大学长期从事对外汉语教学和英语教学的几位教授，对每一集对话进行了加工，增添了生词、注释、替换练习和会话等部分，并负责生词和注释部分的英文翻译。每一集有8～10个生词，有5～8个注释，有模仿练习，也有交际性的活用练习，帮助您更好地理解对话内容，掌握重点词句。

为了适应学习者需要，每册收入15集节目（特殊情况除外），并配有相应拍摄点的简介、图片和旅游资讯。由于节目制作还在进行之中，配套图书将陆续出版。

中国中央电视台中文国际频道

《快乐中国——学汉语》栏目组

PREFACE

The development of China has attracted the attention of the world, as a result of which a great upsurge for learning Chinese has been going on throughout the world.

The CCTV-4 program *Happy China–Learning Chinese* offers learners an opportunity to learn the Chinese language and culture while enjoying the beautiful scenic spots in China. Co-operating with the local administrations of the well-known scenic spots, this program well combines the learning of language skills with that of Chinese culture and history in an interesting, informative and enjoyable way.

With a 98% coverage in the world, the program of CCTV was broadcast since June, 2004. Quite a lot of the viewers expressed the hope to have the language materials as a learning aid. In view of this, we have invited Beijing Language and Culture University Press, a leading press in publications on Chinese learning materials for foreigners, to produce and publish these language materials for our viewers.

Apart from the language materials presented in the program, Words and Expressions, Notes, Substitution Drills and Conversations are provided in each book, among which Words and Expressions and Notes are accompanied with brief English translations or explanations. Each book is composed of about 15 episodes of the TV program with brief introductions and photos of corresponding scenic spots and travel guides. As more episodes of *Happy China–Learning Chinese* are coming up, more books will be published accordingly.

CCTV-4 Happy China--Learning Chinese Production Team

欢乐之城——深圳

深圳是中国南部海滨城市，地处广东省南部，南边的深圳河与香港相连，市区距香港港岛仅45分钟车程。其辽阔的海域连接南海及太平洋，多处可建深水港，水产资源丰富。

Shenzhen —— A City of Joy

Shenzhen, a coastal city in southern China, situates in southern Guangdong Province, connecting Hong Kong through the Shenzhen River in the south. It is only a 45-minute drive from Shenzhen city proper to the island of Hong Kong. Its open sea area links with the South China Sea and the Pacific Ocean. The city is blessed with rich marine resources and great potential for the construction of deepwater wharves.

锦绣中华、中国民俗文化村

在风光旖旎的深圳湾畔，有两颗璀璨的明珠，即两家著名的主题公园——锦绣中华微缩景区、中国民俗文化村。两景区开创了中国主题公园之先河，名声享誉海内外，现已接待中外游客5000多万人次。其中包括世界各地的国家元首、政府首脑、国际知名人士数百人。

2003年元旦，锦绣中华、中国民俗文化村正式合并。

“一步迈进历史，一天游遍中国”，锦绣中华景区浓缩了中国五千年历史文化和全国各地的风景名胜；是一座反映中国历史、文化、古代建筑和民族风情的最丰富、最生动、最全面的实景微缩景区。

“纵览五千年文化，荟萃八万里风情”，中国民俗文化村荟萃了中国各地的服饰、风味、民族建筑及民间艺术风情。景区的民族风情表演独具魅力，激情参与项目惊险刺激，使人流连忘返；大型表演《一代天骄》、《东方霓裳》带给您震撼之余，也让您得到艺术上的享受。

Chinese Folk Culture Theme Park

Splendid China Miniaturc Scenic Spot and Chinese Folk Culture Villages located at the picturesque Shenzhen Bay, are owned and run by Shenzhen Splendid China Development Co., Ltd. They are the earliest and most representative theme parks in China. So far, it has attracted mor than 50 million visitors from all over the world, including hundreds of foreign heads of state, government leaders and international celebrities.

In early 2003, the two theme parks were merged into one comprehensive Chinese Folk Culture Theme Park.

At the Splendid China section, the visitors can virtually set feet in history and tour the whole of China in one single day. This section highlights China's 5,000-year-old history and culture and its various scenic attractions. It is a concentrated display of China's history, culture, architecture and folk customs.

The Chinese Folk Culture Villages section features the costumes of China's various ethnic minorities, their architecture, customs and varieties of folk arts. Here, there are graceful folk dance performances as well as breathtaking games for the visitors. The grand dance performances, "Proud Son of Heaven" and "Oriental Fashions", are purely artistic enjoyment for the visitors.

欢乐谷主题乐园

深圳欢乐谷是一座融参与性、观赏性、娱乐性、趣味性于一体的中国领先的现代主题乐园，集海、陆、空三栖游乐为一身，融日、夜两重娱乐为一体。

全园共分十大主题区：西班牙广场、卡通城、冒险山、欢乐时光、金矿镇、香格里拉森林、飓风湾、阳光海岸、玛雅水公园，还有高空单轨列车“欢乐干线”。

在这里，您可以感受19世纪美国西部的淘金狂潮，进入“世外桃源”并感受寻梦香格里拉的各种神奇经历，领略玛雅文明的神奇，体验浓郁的加勒比海湾风情和欧洲小镇嘉年华的热闹繁华。在这里，您可以在丛林绿荫里穿行飞跃，在雨林中分享奇妙，在娱乐中体验冒险的真实，在自然中感受返璞归真的野趣。在这里，您可以体验一百多个老少皆宜、丰富多彩的游乐项目。您可以领略到国内第一座“悬挂式过山车”的惊险，体验“天旋地转”的“飞”一般的感觉，感受“龙卷风”灵魂出窍的刺激，经历“激流勇进”飞流直下的难忘历程……还有太空梭、矿山车、发现者、UFO、四维电影、风情歌舞等更多的精彩内容。

一次次惊心动魄的欢乐历程，一个个亦真亦幻的欢乐世界，中国最具魅力的都市娱乐中心，一个“动感、时尚、欢乐、梦幻”的繁华都市，将让你永志难忘！

Happy Valley Theme Park

Happy Valley Theme Park in Shenzhen is one of China's leading modern theme parks incorporating visitor participation, sightseeing, entertainment and amusement. Visitors here have access to amusement activities carried out in the sea, on the land and in the air. It is open day and night.

The park is divided into ten theme sections: Spanish Plaza, Cartoon City, Adventure Hill, Happy Time, Gold Mine Town, Shangri La Forest, Hurricane Bay, Sunshine Beach, the Maya Aquatic Park and the monorail Happy Rail.

Here, the visitor can virtually experience the Gold Rush of the 19th century American West, the Shangri La dreamland, the magical Maya civilization and the flavors of the Caribbean region and the hustle and bustle of small European towns. The visitor can travel through a rain forest and experience the thrilling outdoor adventures and enjoy over 100 amusement activities, which are suitable both for children and adults. They include a ride on the country's latest state-of-the-art roller coaster and the breathtaking experiences of a tornado, a splashing boat ride, Space Shuttle Discovery, UFOs and four-dimensional films, as well as a myriad of other fun items that cater to the visitors'curiosity and quest for adventure.

The various entertaining items bring you into a fun world of thrills and excitement, an unforgettable fantasyland of action,fashion, gaiety and adventure in this most glamorous Chinese city of Shenzhen.

世界之窗

1994年开业的中国深圳世界之窗，坐落于美丽的中国深圳湾畔，占地48万平方米。景区按世界地域结构和游览活动内容分为世界广场、亚洲区、大洋洲区、欧洲区、非洲区、美洲区、世界雕塑园和国际街八大区域。作为以弘扬世界文化精华为主题的大型文化旅游景区，它荟萃了众多世界著名景观，集自然风光、民俗风情、民间歌舞、大型演出以及高科技参与性娱乐项目于一园，再现了一个美妙的世界。

游，有130个不同比例的逼真的世界著名景观，让游客尽览世界精彩；玩，有集高科技和文化主题于一体的十大参与性娱乐项目，让游客放纵飞扬激情；赏，有鸿篇巨制大型晚会《千古风流》，让游客感受恢弘壮丽的艺术震撼；乐，有尽显世界民俗风情的主题活动，让游客领略不同文化的异彩纷呈；住，有位于欧风街上美景与舒适相融的城市客栈，让游客尽情享受。

“您给我一天，我给您一个世界”，这就是深圳世界之窗对全世界朋友的承诺。

深圳，一个永远带给人们欢乐的城市。

Window of the World

Opened up in 1994, Shenzhen's Window of the World, lies near the scenic Shenzhen Bay area and covers a total area of 480,000 square meters. Based on geographic structure and tourist attractions, the park is divided into eight sections: the World Square, Asia, Oceania, Europe, Africa, the Americas, and the World Sculpture Garden and the International streets. As a world multi-cultural theme park, Window of the World features the world's major tourist attractions, natural scenery, folk customs and folk dances. With hi-tech means, the park is intended to presents the world scenic attractions to the visitors in a miniature manner.

There are 130 vivid replicas of famous world sites of cultural and historical interests for sightseeing. Ten major recreational activities combining hi-tech with cultural themes provide the visitors with utmost excitement. There are also a grand evening performance "Charms from the Past" and displays of folk customs from all over the world. Besides visitors can be accommodated in posh European-style hotels.

A day at the Window of the World will enable the visitors to see virtually all parts of the world.

Shenzhen a city that will always bring fun and joy to all visitors.

目录

CONTENTS

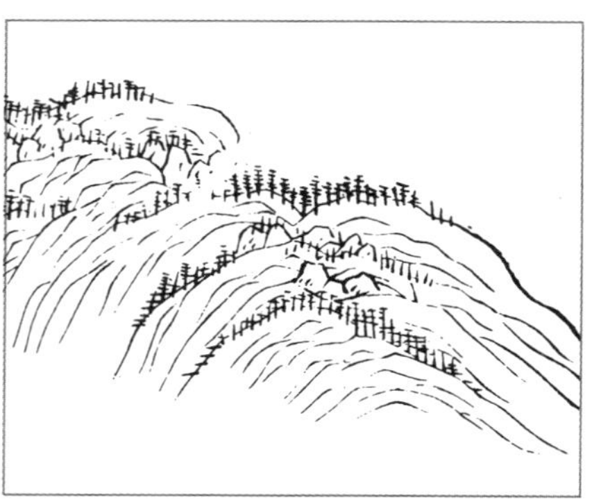

民俗村
【第一集】

场景 Scene　民俗村

韩　佳：今天啊，我们要去深圳的民俗村转转。这民俗村啊……

大　牛：民俗村哪？韩佳，不愧为我的搭档，就是了解我[1]。中国各个地区的民风民俗我特别感兴趣。你赶快带我去转转吧！

韩　佳：好，那我先问问你，什么是民风民俗？

大　牛：就是民间风尚、风俗习惯呗！包括衣、食、住、行，还有……

韩　佳：好，那我们今天就找这里的衣、食、住、行。咱俩分头把这里最有特色的衣、食、住、行找出来，怎么样？

大　牛：还要找啊？

Han Jia: Today, we are going to visit the Chinese Folk Culture Villages in Shenzhen. Folk Culture Villages ...

Daniel: Folk Culture Villages? Han Jia is a real partner. She knows me well. I am very interested in folk culture of various areas in China. Hurry up! Take me to have a look.

Han Jia: OK. I'd like to ask you first what folk culture is.

Daniel: Folk habits and customs, including food, clothing, shelter and means of travelling, and ...

Han Jia: OK. Let's look for "yi shi zhu xing" here today, and find out the most characteristic "yi shi zhu xing" here.

Daniel: Look for them?

场景 Scene 藤桥

韩　佳：这么快我就发现了一处，这是我国云南兄弟民族村寨中常见的一种藤桥，是用藤和铁索制成的。这样既结实耐用，又方便人们出行。②

Tā jì jiēshi nàiyòng, yòu fāngbiàn rénmen chūxíng.

它 既 结实 耐用，又 方便 人们 出行。

It's both sturdy and convenient.

大　牛：韩佳，你真行啊！你一下子就找到了衣食住行中的“行”。

韩　佳：大牛，你也不错啊！一句话里面说了一个多义词，表达了两种意思。

大　牛：多义词？

韩　佳：对呀，就是“行”。“行”的基本意思是行走，比如说：人行道、旅行。它也可以泛指跟交通有关的，比如刚才我们所说的衣食住行的“行”。当然了，它也可以用来夸奖别人，就像大牛刚才夸奖我：“你真行！”那就是在说我非常能干。

Han Jia: Found a place so soon. This is a common rattan bridge in villages of ethnic groups in Yunnan Province. It is made of rattan and iron chain. It is a solid, durable and convenient means of travelling.

Daniel: Han Jia, you are capable to find the means of travelling quickly.

Han Jia: Daniel, you are pretty good to use a polysemic word to express two meanings.

Daniel: Polysemic word?

Han Jia: Yes. It is "xing". The basic meaning of "xing" is to walk. For example, "ren xingdao, lüxing". It can be used to refer to things concerning traffic. Such as "yi shi zhu xing" we just mentioned. It can be also used to compliment others. Just now, Daniel complimented me "Ni zhen xing", which means that "you are very capable".

场景 Scene　品尝土家腊肉

韩　佳：大牛，这么快就累了？

大　牛：累倒不累，我就是肚子有点饿。③

韩　佳：又想吃了？

大　牛：你先别急着说我，我这不是要完成一项任务吗？这里就是衣食住行中的“食”。

商　贩：土家的腊肉真好吃啊，好吃啊！过来！请慢用！

合：谢谢。

韩　佳：大牛，你可真是工作吃饭两不误啊！这不但闻起来很香，吃起来还有股特别的辣味儿，味道好极了！④

Tā chī qilai hái yǒu yì gǔ tèbié de là wèr.

它吃起来还有一股特别的辣味儿。

There is a unique spicy flavour to it.

Han Jia: Daniel, are you tired?

Daniel: No. I am a little hungry.

Han Jia: Are you hungry again?

Daniel: Don't be anxious to blame me. It's a task. The "shi" in "yi shi zhu xing".

The Peddler : Cured meat is delicious. Please enjoy your meal.

Together : Thank you.

Han Jia: Daniel, you indeed never miss your work and meal. It not only smells good, but also has a special hot taste. Very delicious.

民俗村

场景 Scene 窑洞前

大　牛：韩佳。

韩　佳：大牛，你带我来的这个地方还真有特色。

大　牛：那当然。

韩　佳：这是哪儿啊？

大　牛：这个，我还真不知道。

韩　佳：不知道我就告诉你。这里是陕西的窑洞，是当地最有特色的民居。

大　牛：那里的人怎么要住在洞里啊？

韩　佳：是窑洞。窑洞里非常舒服。陕西在我国北方的黄土高原上，一山接着一山，黄土连着黄土，所以当地的人就因地制宜，在山崖畔凿出土窑洞来。

大　牛：这可真是靠山吃山，靠水吃水。

韩　佳：这可不叫靠山吃山，这叫靠山住山。你呀，不要小瞧这窑洞。住在里面冬暖夏凉，而且这样的顶不容易塌陷。

大　牛：这窑洞虽然看着不起眼，但是还挺科学呀！⑤那里的人可真聪明！

韩　佳：那当然了，黄河儿女嘛，脑子里都是智慧。他们不仅心灵，而且手巧。

Tāmen bùjǐn xīnlíng, érqiě shǒu qiǎo

他们 不仅 心灵，而且 手 巧。

Not only are they highly intelligent, they are skilled workers as well.

Daniel: Han Jia.

Han Jia: Daniel, this place is very unique.

Daniel: Of course.

Han Jia: What is it?

Daniel: I don't know.

Han Jia: I can tell you. It's a "yaodong" of Shaanxi Province, the most characteristic civilian residence of the local people.

Daniel: Why do they live in the cave?

Han Jia: It's a "yaodong". It's comfortable to live in "yaodong". Shaanxi is on the Loess Plateau in North China, where there are continuous mountains and vast loess. So local people adap to local conditions to dig caves in the cliff.

Daniel: It's "kao shan chi shan, kao shui chi shui".

Han Jia: It's "kao shan zhu shan" instead of "kao shan chi shan". Don't disdain the "yaodong". It's warm in winter and cool in summer to live in, and such ceiling doesn't collapse easily.

Daniel: It looks unimportant but in fact scientific. The local people are very smart.

Han Jia: Of course. They are offsprings of the Yellow River who are full of wisdom. They are quick-witted and nimble-fingered.

中国 场景 Scene 民俗村

大　牛：韩佳，怎么是你啊？你怎么这身打扮？

韩　佳：认不出来了吧？⑥这是白族姑娘的服饰。

大　牛：不错，不错！刚才我还真没认出来。你怎么好像一下子高了很多啊？对了，就是这顶帽子的缘故。

韩　佳：这帽子特别吧？它不仅外形很特别，意义也很特别，代表了风花雪月四种自然景观。大牛，你来找找！

大　牛：这个花最简单，这一朵一朵就是。上面这排白白的就是雪啊！可是风和月呢？我找不着。

韩　佳：还是让我来告诉你吧！这长长的穗子就代表风，而帽子弯弯的形状就代表月。风花雪月是世间美好的事物，它代表了白族姑娘美丽的外表和纯洁的心灵。

大　牛：没想到一顶帽子还有这么多美好的含义。中国民俗真是丰富多彩啊！

韩　佳：好了，衣、食、住、行，今天我们都找到了，节目结束的时间也要到了⑦。

大　牛：可是还有很多新奇有意思的我们还没有转到呢！

韩　佳：没关系，明天接着转！

Daniel: Han Jia, it's you! Why do you dress up like this?

Han Jia: Can't you recognize me? It's a dress of girls of Bai ethnic group.

Daniel: It's nice. I could hardly recognize you just now. You look much taller. Yes, because of this hat.

Han Jia: Is it special? It has a special shape and special meanings, representing four natural scenes of wind, flowers, snow and moon. Daniel, look for them.

Daniel: Flowers are the easiest to find. Here, one after another. This white decoration is snow. But I can't find wind and moon.

Han Jia: Let me tell you. The long tassel represents wind, and the crescent shape represents the moon. "Feng hua xue yue" refers to beautiful things in the world. It symbolizes beautiful appearances and pure hearts of girls of Bai ethnic group.

Daniel: Little did I think that a hat contains so many good meanings. Chinese folk culture is really colorful.

Han Jia: Well, we have found today's "yi shi zhu xing". And it's time to wrap up for today.

Daniel: But there are many other interesting places we haven't visited.

Han Jia: Don't worry. We'll continue tomorrow.

生词 New Words and Expressions

1.	不愧	(副)	búkuì	creditably
2.	结实	(形)	jiēshi	firm and strong
3.	耐用	(形)	nàiyòng	durable
4.	包括	(动)	bāokuò	to include
5.	特色	(名)	tèsè	characteristic
6.	旅行	(动、名)	lǚxíng	to travel; travel
7.	夸奖	(动)	kuājiǎng	to praise
8.	着急	(形)	zháojí	to be anxious
9.	任务	(名)	rènwu	task
10.	心灵手巧		xīn líng shǒu qiǎo	clever and deft

注释 Notes

1. 不愧为我的搭档，就是了解我。

“就是”，副词，强调肯定，确实如此。

“就是”，an adverb, is used to emphasize affirmation.

例如：这里的饭菜就是好吃。

2. 这样既结实耐用，又方便人们出行。

“既……又……”这一结构表示同时具有两个方面的性质或情况。

The structure “既……又……” indicates that both situations or characteristics are available.

例如：他既聪明又努力，每次考试都考得很好。

3. 累倒不累，我就是肚子有点饿。

“形容词＋倒不＋形容词……就是……”这一结构，“倒”表示一种让步，“就是”起转折作用，引出另一件事。

In the structure “adjective+ 倒不＋adjective……就是……”,“倒” indicates concession, while “就是” makes the transition, leading to another thing or matter.

例如：路倒不远，就是路不平，不好走。

4．味道好**极了**。

“形容词＋极了”这一结构表示最高程度，常用于口语。

The structure “adjective＋极了” indicates the highest degree, often used in spoken Chinese.

例如：今天的天气好极了，我们出去玩儿玩儿吧！

5．这窑洞**虽然**看着不起眼，**但是**还挺科学呀！

“虽然……但是……”表示转折，“虽然”说出一个事实，“但是”引出的是一个相反的事实。

“虽然……但是……” is a transitional complex sentence structure, in which “虽然” indicates a fact while “但是” introduces a contrary fact.

例如：他虽然会说一些汉语，但是要当一名汉语翻译还不行。

6．认不**出来**了吧？

在这里，“出来”用在动词后，表示人或事物随动作由隐蔽到显露，“认不出来”意思是不认识了。

“出来” added to a verb is used to express the idea that something or some person appears from obscurity with the action. “认不出来” means “cannot recognize (you)”.

例如：几年不见，刚才你叫我，我都认不出来是你了。

7．节目结束的时间也**要**到**了**。

“要……了”这一结构表示动作、情况很快将要发生或出现。基本句式为：

The expression “要……了” means some action or event is going to happen. Its basic structure is:

主语	要	谓语动词	宾语	了
Subject	要	Predicate verb	Object	了
节目结束的时间	要	到		了。
他们	要	上	课	了。

为强调时间紧迫，还可以在“要”前加副词“就”“快”，也可以只用“快……了”。

例如：飞机就要起飞了。

火车快要到了。

我们快放假了。

Sometimes in order to emphasize the immediacy, “就” or “快” is added in front of “要”, and also “快……了” can be used instead.

“要……了”和“就要……了”前面可以加表示具体时间的词语做状语。“快要……了”和“快……了”不能加。

Adverbials of time can be added in front of “要……了” and “就要……了” whereas “快要……了” and “快……了” cannot be used with adverbials of time.

例如：八点钟银行要开门了。

明天他们就要回国了。

否定式用“还没(有)……呢”。

In its negative form, “还没（有）……呢” is often used.

例如：他们还没睡觉呢。

替换练习 Substitution Drills

1. 它既	结实耐用，	又方便人们	出行。
	营养丰富		食用
	美观实用		携带
	物美价廉		使用

2. 它	吃	起来还有一	股	特别的	辣味儿。
	吹		种		声音
	闻		种		香味儿
	摸		种		感觉

3. 他们不仅	心灵，	而且	手巧。
	会唱		会跳
	懂英语		懂汉语
	是师生		是朋友

会话 Conversations

完成下列对话　Complete the following dialogues
（如括号里有词语或提示，请按要求做　Use the words or phrases given in the brackets）

A: 走了半天了，你饿不饿？

B: ________________。（……倒不……，就是……）

A: 那就休息一会儿吧。

B: 好，休息一会儿吧。

A: 这个礼物怎么样？

B: 不错。贵吗？

A: 很便宜。

B: ________________，我也去买一个。（既……又……）

民俗村
【第二集】

场景 Scene 民俗村内

大　牛：这是什么东西？真好玩。

韩　佳：少见多怪了吧。这是民间的一种土电话。用一根棉线把两个小竹筒连接起来，就可以传声了。我小的时候就玩儿过。①

大　牛：嘿，真新鲜，回去我也做一个玩儿玩儿。

韩　佳：你昨天不是说了吗？②要找新奇有意思的东西。那我今天就带你去找找“新、奇、有意思”。

Daniel: What's this? So funny.

Han Jia: You consider it funny because you've never seen it before. It's a folk telephone made up of two small bamboo tubes linked by a cotton tread. I once played it when I was a kid.

Daniel: Hey, it's novel. I'll make one myself.

Han Jia: Didn't you say yesterday you would find interesting things? I'll take you to find something interesting.

场景 Scene 纳西族民居前

大　牛：韩佳，别人的对联都写字，这户人家的对联怎么画画呢？
韩　佳：新鲜吧？其实这不是画，而是一种文字。③

Zhè bú shì huà, ér shì yì zhǒng wénzì.

这 不 是 画，而 是 一 种 文字。

These aren't drawings, they are words.

韩　佳：这是中国的纳西族东巴文字，已经有几千年的历史了。
大　牛：能保存到现在真不容易啊！
韩　佳：的确挺不容易的。这是一种古老的象形文字，仅有两千一百多个，但是却撰写出了一千四百多种东巴经典，而且至今还有人在用呢！
大　牛：确实不简单！不过你别光顾着给我们大家介绍，你倒是告诉我这上面写的是什么啊④？
韩　佳：刚才我说了，这是象形文字。那你就看看它的形状，猜猜呗！
大　牛：我猜这上面的就是老鹰，最后一个字应该是鱼，所以这个念："老鹰捉小鱼"。
韩　佳：大牛，你也太离谱儿了吧？
大　牛：什么谱啊？
韩　佳：离谱儿啊！这是一句口语，就是说你猜的和实际的相差太远。来，我告诉你，记好了！
大　牛：好！
韩　佳：这边是：虎来赠山月，那边是：鹤来赐云福。横批是：长寿富裕。

Daniel: Han Jia. People usually write characters on couplet, but this family drew on the couplet.

Han Jia: Strange? Actually, it's not a drawing, but a kind of characters.

Han Jia: These are Dongba characters of Naxi ethnic group of China with a history of several thousand years.

Daniel: It's uneasy to come down to present days.

Han Jia: Very difficult, indeed. It is a kind of ancient pictograph. It has only about two thousand and one hundred characters, but had been used to write more than one thousand and four hundred Dongba classics, and is still in use today.

Daniel: It's great. Don't merely introduce it to us, please tell me what these characters mean.

Han Jia: I told you it is a kind of pictograph. Then you can guess according to the shapes.

Daniel: I guess the one above is an eagle, the last one should be a fish. So it is an eagle diving down on a fish.

Han Jia: Daniel, you are too "lipur".

Daniel: What "pu"?

Han Jia: "Lipur". A colloquial phrase which means what you guessed is far from the truth. Well, I'll tell you. You remember it.

Daniel: Yes.

Han Jia: The first line is: Tiger presents mountain and moon; the second is: Crane bestows clouds and fortune. The horizontal scroll is: Longevity and prosperity.

民俗村

场景 Scene 侗寨

大　牛：韩佳，这是什么地方啊？这梯子上怎么全是刀啊？

韩　佳：大牛，瞧把你吓的。这里是侗族人过节举行活动的地方。今天你可算是来对了，一会儿就有这寨子里的人要举行上刀山表演。

大　牛：上刀山！

韩　佳：你没有听说过一句俗语叫"上刀山，下火海"吗？

shàng dāo shān, xià huǒ hǎi

上刀山，下火海

To do something extremely dangerous.

韩　佳：这刀山、火海是指非常艰险的地方。敢于上刀山、下火海的行为被视为是一种非常英勇的表现。

大　牛：上刀山，下火海，形容去做非常艰险的事情。

韩　佳：没错，就是这个意思。在中国的兄弟民族中，就有用锋利的刀搭起来的刀梯。有人会从下面一步一步地登上去，而不割破手脚。你信不信？

大　牛：这可是真功夫啊，我得好好见识见识！

韩　佳：你看，他们来了！

Daniel: Han Jia, where are we? Why are there so many knives on the ladder?

Han Jia: Daniel, don't be afraid. People of Dong ethnic group hold activities here during festivals. You are fortunate to be here today, because the villagers will present a performance named "shang dao shan".

Daniel: "Shang dao shan"!

Han Jia: Have you ever heard a common saying "Shang dao shan, xia huo hai"? "Dao shan" and "huo hai" refer to very dangerous places. The courage to "shang dao shan" and "xia huo hai" is regarded as a very heroic performance.

Daniel: Climbing up a mountain of daggers and diving into a sea of flames is a metaphor for doing something which is incredibly dangerous.

Han Jia: Yes, that's right. Some ethnic groups of China still have ladders built of sharp knives. Some people can climb up the ladder step by step without lacerating their hands and feet. Do you believe it?

Daniel: That's real Kungfu. I'll witness it personally.

Han Jia: Look! Here they are.

场景 Scene 佤寨

大　牛：韩佳，我们这是来到了哪儿？怎么到处都挂着牛头啊？

韩　佳：这个地方你才该来呢，这里是佤寨。佤族人有两大特点，第一，就是在门口挂牛头。谁家门口挂的牛头最大，就说明谁家最有钱、最有地位。⑤你来这里呀，肯定受欢迎。

大　牛：那不错啊，牛的地位还挺高嘛！那第二呢？

韩　佳：第二嘛，你看！

大　牛：那个人怎么长得这么黑呀？⑥

韩　佳：那是佤族人，佤族人崇尚黑色。

Wǎzúrén chóngshàng hēisè.

佤族人　崇尚　黑色。

The Wa ethnic group adore the color black.

韩　佳：佤族人崇尚黑色，人长得越黑就越漂亮⑦。像你这么白的嘛……

大　牛：我去晒晒太阳还不行啊！

场景 Scene 佤寨歌舞

韩　佳：今天真是太高兴了！这佤寨里的人们真是太可爱了！

大　牛：我大牛和这位 Mr.Chocolate 已经成为很好的朋友了。

Daniel: Han Jia. Where are we now? There are so many ox heads hanging here and there.

Han Jia: It's the very place you should come. It is a Village of Wa ethnic group.The Wa people have two characteristics. The first one is to hang ox heads at the gate. The biggest ox head indicates the richest and most powerful family. So you are welcome here for certain.

Daniel: That's not bad. Ox has such a high status. How about the second?

Han Jia: The second? Look!

Daniel: That man is so dark.

Han Jia: He is the person of Wa ethnic group. The Wa people regard black as a fashion.

Han Jia: The people of Wa ethnic group regard black as a fashion. The darker, the more beautiful. For those as white as you ...

Daniel: I'll take sunbaths.

Han Jia: I am so happy today. The people in Wa's Village are very lovely.

Daniel: Mr.Chocolate and I have become good friends.

生词 New Words and Expressions

1. 好玩儿	（形）	hǎowánr	amusing, funny, interesting
2. 保存	（动）	bǎocún	to keep
3. 赠	（动）	zèng	to give as a present
4. 富裕	（形）	fùyù	abundant
5. 举行	（动）	jǔxíng	to hold
6. 艰险	（形）	jiānxiǎn	hard and dangerous
7. 英勇	（形）	yīngyǒng	heroic, courageous
8. 见识	（动、名）	jiànshi	to learn; knowledge
9. 肯定	（动、形）	kěndìng	to confirm; affirmative
10. 崇尚	（动）	chóngshàng	to uphold, advocate

注释 Notes

1. 我小的时候就玩儿过。

"过"，动态助词，用在动词或少数形容词之后，表示过去曾经有过某种经历。基本句式为：

"过"，an auxiliary word, is used after a verb and sometimes a few adjectives, expressing the idea that "something has been done before". Its basic pattern is：

主语——谓语动词（形容词）—— 过——宾语

Subject----Predicate verb/Adjective---- 过 ---- Object

我　　玩儿　　过。

我们　　看　　过　　这部电影。

否定式用"没有"。

In the negative form "没有" is used in front of the predicate verb.

例如：我没有见过这个人，我不认识他。

2. 你昨天不是说了吗？

"不是……吗"这是一个反问句，用否定形式表示肯定的看法。

"不是……吗" is a rhetorical question form, used to indicate positive attitude.

例如：他不是去上海了吗？（他去上海了。）

3. **其实这不是画，而是一种文字。**

"其实"，副词，表示所说的情况是真实的。

"其实", an adverb, is used to mean what is said is true.

例如：我只是听人说过，其实我不认识他。

"不是……而是……"这一结构表示否定前者，肯定后者。

In this structure, the former is negated while the latter is affirmed.

例如：他不是英国人而是美国人。

4. **你倒是告诉我这上面写的是什么啊？**

"倒是"，副词，表示催促、追问。

"倒是", an adverb, is used to mean to urge or to question closely.

例如：你倒是快点儿啊，马上就要上课了。

5. **谁家门口挂的牛头最大，就说明谁家最有钱、最有地位。**

"谁……谁……"是疑问代词的一种任指用法。第一个疑问代词是任指的，随便哪一个人；第二个疑问代词是以第一个疑问代词为转移的，指同一个人。

"谁……谁……" is an arbitrary use of interrogative pronouns with the first one as an arbitrary pronoun, referring to "any one" while the second depends on the first, referring to the same person.

例如：学校下星期有书法比赛，谁想参加谁就去报名。

6. **那个人怎么长得这么黑呀？**

在这个句子中，"这么黑"是补充说明动词"长"的程度。这种补充说明动作达到的程度的成分，称为程度补语。程度补语和动词之间要用结构助词"得"来连接。基本句式为：

In this sentence, "这么黑" is used to complement the degree of the verb "长". Words like this are called complement of degree. "得" is used to link the complement of degree and the verb. Its basic sentence pattern is:

主语——谓语动词（形容词）——得——程度补语

Subject---- Predicate verb------------- 得 -----Complement of degree

他　　　　跑　　　　　　得　　真快。

他　　　　说　　　　　　得　　很好。

否定式是在程度补语之前加“不”。

“不” is added in front of the complement of degree to make up the negative form.

例如：他唱得不好。

如果既有宾语，又有程度补语，一般要重复动词。

The verb is usually repeated if it takes an object and a complement of degree.

例如：他说汉语说得很流利。

7．人长得越黑就越漂亮。

“越A越B”这一结构表示在程度上B随A的增加而增加，A和B可以是同一个主语，也可以分属两个主语。

The structure “越A越B” indicates the degree of B is increased with A' s increase. A and B can share the same subject and they can also have two different subjects.

例如：这本小说太有意思了，我越看越想看。

你别说了，你越说，他越生气。

替换练习 Substitution Drills

1．这不是　画，　而是一　种　文字。

马　　　　头　驴

客车　　　辆　货车

油画　　　幅　中国画

2．上　刀山　下　火海。

北京　　广州

传　　　达

窜　　　跳

3. 佤族人　　崇尚　　黑色
　唐朝妇女　　　　　丰满
　姑娘　　　　　　　美容
　清朝皇帝　　　　　黄色

会话 Conversations

完成下列对话　Complete the following dialogues
（如括号里有词语或提示，请按要求做　Use the words or phrases given in the brackets）

A: 你墙上的这幅山水画不错。

B: ______________。（不是……，而是……）

A: 是照片？有多少年了？

B: 有二三十年了。

A: 这家商店的顾客是不是太多了？

B: 对商店来说______________。（越……越……）

A: 是啊！

B: 顾客多，商店赚的钱就会更多。

民俗村

【第三集】

场景 Scene 傣家象脚鼓前

大　牛：今天……这是谁在这里给我捣乱呢？原来是你呀！①

韩　佳：对呀！观众朋友们，大家好，我是快乐的韩佳！

大　牛：韩佳，你干吗跟我捣乱呢？

韩　佳：这哪是捣乱啊？敲傣家的象脚鼓是表示祝福的意思。今天我们要去找乐器，这民俗村里的民间乐器可多着呢②，我们去看看！

大　牛：好！

Daniel: Today, who's doing that? It's you!

Han Jia: Yes. Hello, audience friends. I am Merry Han Jia.

Daniel: Han Jia. Why did you make trouble?

Han Jia: I didn't. Beating Elephant-foot Drum of Dai ethnic group is a way to express good wishes. Today, we are going to look for musical instruments. There are so many folk musical instruments in the Folk Culture Villages. Let's go and take a look.

Daniel: OK.

民俗村

场景 Scene 民俗村内

大　牛：韩佳，这是乐器吗？不就是什么瓦缸、竹筒之类的吗？③

韩　佳：怎么，你不服气啊？那你倒是敲出个“多来咪”让我来听听。

大　牛：别说“多来咪”，就是“咪来多”我都能给你敲回来。④

韩　佳：大牛，你还真有长进，刚才还用了个“别说”。那你知道它是什么意思吗？

大　牛：“别说”就是不要说话的意思呗！

韩　佳：“别说”在这个句子中是一个连词，表示递进关系，为了降低某一事物的重要性，借以突出另一事物的重要性。我们还可以说“别说这点儿小事儿了，就是再难的事儿大牛都能解决”。

Biéshuō zhè diǎn xiǎo shì, zài nán de shì tā dōu néng jiějué.

别说这点小事，再难的事他都能解决。

These trivialities are nothing,
even the hardest problems are easy for him to solve.

大　牛：韩佳，你有什么困难的事，尽管说吧！

韩　佳：说了那么多啊，我有点口渴了，你去给我找点水来。

大　牛：好嘞！

韩　佳：今天他怎么那么痛快啊？

Daniel: Han Jia. Is this a musical instrument? It's just something like pottery jars and bamboo tubes.

Han Jia: Don't you believe? Can you play Do-Re-Mi with it?

Daniel: Let alone Do-Re-Mi, I can play Mi-Re-Do, too.

Han Jia: Daniel, you made progress. You used "bieshuo" just now. Do you know the meaning?

Daniel: "Bieshuo" means "don't speak".

Han Jia: "Bieshuo" is a conjunction in this sentence, which express progressive relationship by lowering importance of one thing to give emphasis on another. We can say "Bieshuo zhe dian xiao shi le, jiushi zai da de shi Daniel dou neng jiejue".

Daniel: Han Jia. If you have difficulties, don't hesitate to tell me.

Han Jia: We've talked for a while. I feel thirsty. Can you fetch me some water?

Daniel: No problem.

Han Jia: Why is he so kind today?

场景 Scene 水车前

韩　佳：大牛，水呢？

大　牛：这不就是水吗？

韩　佳：这就是你给我找的水啊？这水能喝吗？

大　牛：韩佳，你先别生气呀！这水是不能喝，但是能听啊！你听这“叮叮咚咚”的，多好听啊！怎么样？我找的这件乐器不错吧？

韩　佳：乐器？你看，你又犯自以为是的毛病了吧？这哪是乐器啊？⑤ 这是用来赶鸟的。

大　牛：赶鸟的？

韩　佳：对呀，因为鸟到处啄食，破坏了田里的庄稼，于是，人们就利用水的落差和竹筒，做出了这样一个东西，能发出“叮叮咚咚”的声音来，鸟一听就被吓跑了。

大　牛：还真有创意呀！

Zhè hái zhēn yǒu chuàngyì.

这 还 真 有 创意。

This is quite creative.

韩　佳：大牛，想卖弄一下，结果又演砸了吧？

Han Jia: Daniel, where is my water?

Daniel: Isn't it water?

Han Jia: Is it the water for me? Is it drinkable?

Daniel: Han Jia. Don't be angry. It's undrinkable but listenable. Listen to the clinking music. How about it? I found a nice musical instrument.

Han Jia: Musical instrument? You self-righteous guy. It is not a musical instrument, but a device to disperse birds.

Daniel: Disperse birds?

Han Jia: Yes. Birds peck and destroy crops in the farmland everywhere. So people use the drop of water and bamboo tube to make such a device to scare the birds away by the clinking sound.

Daniel: It's really creative.

Han Jia: Daniel. You failed to show off again.

场景 Scene 彝族村寨

大　牛：韩佳，刚才你说我什么？你说我卖什么？把什么给砸了呀？

韩　佳：刚才我说你"卖弄"。"卖弄"就是指故意炫耀自己的本事。还有"砸"，除了有你知道的撞击、打破东西以外，还有失败的意思⑥。说你"演砸了"就是说你卖弄失败了。

大　牛：你瞧瞧你这个人，老说我。

韩　佳：你听，怎么那么热闹？我们过去看看。

大　牛：走！

场景 Scene 彝族村寨

大　牛：韩佳，这些不都是劳动用的工具吗？还有我大牛爱吃的玉米，是乐器吗？

韩　佳：这些东西到了彝族人的手中就成了乐器了。他们在劳动中发现不同的劳动工具可以发出不同的声音，于是就把节奏、音律组合在了一起，形成了美妙的音乐。

大　牛：那他们就可以一边劳动，一边自娱自乐了。⑦

Tāmen kěyǐ yìbiān láodòng, yìbiān zì yú zì lè.

他们 可以 一边 劳动，一边 自 娱 自 乐。

They enjoy themselves as they work.

Daniel: Han Jia. What did you say? What I sold and smashed?

Han Jia: I said you "mainong". "Mainong" means to show off. In addition to striking or breaking something, "za" also means failing to do something. "Yan za le" means you failed to show off.

Daniel: Look at yourself. You always blame me.

Han Jia: Listen! It's so noisy! Let's go and take a look.

Daniel: Let's go!

Daniel: Han Jia. Aren't they instruments of labor? And the corn Daniel loves to eat. Are they musical instruments?

Han Jia: In the hands of Yi nationality people, they become musical instruments. These people found that different instruments of labor make different sounds. So they compose the rhythms and melodies into enjoyable music.

Daniel: Therefore, they can entertain themselves while working.

场景 Scene 民俗村内

韩　佳：陈先生，你好。
陈先生：你好。
韩　佳：我是《快乐中国》的韩佳，我今天带大牛来见识见识咱们中国的笛子。
陈先生：好啊！笛子是我们中国民族乐器中的一块瑰宝。
大　牛：真了不起！这个笛子有多长啊？
陈先生：这有1米2。
大　牛：比一般的笛子长出好几倍呢！
韩　佳：刚才吹得非常好听，可是吹着费力吗？
陈先生：这个不用费力，一般有一定的功底就能吹了。
大　牛：那有没有更费力气的？
陈先生：有，还有那个3米2的大笛子。这是龙笛。
大　牛：这么长啊！这可怎么吹啊？
陈先生：这个是一个人吹，两个人摁孔。
大　牛：有没有短一点的？
陈先生：还有世界上最小的笛子。
韩　佳：最小的？
大　牛：我们看看。
韩　佳：那么小，好像只有几厘米。瞧瞧，大牛都听入神了。

Han Jia: Hello, Mr. Chen.

Mr. Chen : Hello.

Han Jia: I am Han Jia from Happy China. Today, I take Daniel here to learn something about Chinese flute.

Mr. Chen : OK. Flute is a treasure in Chinese folk musical instruments.

Daniel: It' s great. How long is this flute?

Mr. Chen : It is 1.2-meter long.

Daniel: It is several times longer than normal flutes.

Han Jia: You played excellent, but is it difficult to play?

Mr. Chen : Not at all. You can play it with basic training.

Daniel: Is there any one more difficult to play?

Mr. Chen : Yes. This one is 3.2-meter long. It is called Dragon Flute.

Daniel: Such a long flute. How do you play it?

Mr. Chen : One person plays, while two people press the holes.

Daniel: Are there smaller ones?

Mr. Chen : Yes. We have the smallest flute in the world.

Han Jia: Smallest?

Daniel: Let us have a look.

Han Jia: Only a few centimeters long. Look! Daniel is enthralled.

生词 New Words and Expressions

1.	捣乱	（动）	dǎoluàn	to make trouble
2.	祝福	（动）	zhùfú	to wish one good luck
3.	乐器	（名）	yuèqì	musical instrument
4.	服气	（动）	fúqì	to be convinced
5.	解决	（动）	jiějué	to solve
6.	尽管	（连）	jǐnguǎn	although, in spite of
7.	痛快	（形）	tòngkuai	joyful, straightforward
8.	创意	（名）	chuàngyì	creative ideas
9.	自娱自乐		zì yú zì lè	to amuse oneself
10.	瑰宝	（名）	guībǎo	treasure

注释 Notes

1. 原来是你呀！

“原来”，副词，发现从前不知道的情况，含有恍然醒悟的意思。

“原来”，an adverb, means to discover what is not known before, implying the idea of “seeing the truth all of a sudden”.

例如：这几天没见到他，原来他病了。

2. 这民俗村里的民间乐器可多着呢！

“着呢”，助词，用在形容词或形容词词组之后，表示程度高，有夸张的意味，多用于口语。

“着呢”，an auxiliary word, is used after an adjective or an adjectival phrase, indicating a high degree, and with a bit of exaggeration. It is often used in spoken Chinese.

例如：东北冬天的天气冷着呢。

3. 不就是什么瓦缸、竹筒之类的吗？

“什么”用在几个并列成分前表示列举。

"什么" used before several parallel elements indicates enumeration.

例如：桌子上什么书啊、报纸啊、铅笔啊、尺子啊，摆得满满的。

4. 别说"多来咪"，就是"咪来多"我都能给你敲回来。

"别说"，连词，用于降低所要叙述的事情的重要性，以便突出"就是"引出的事情的重要性。

"别说"，a conjunction, is used to lessen the importance of the thing narrated, so as to emphasize what is led to by "就是".

例如：这种啤酒别说是两杯，就是五杯我也能喝下去。

5. 这哪是乐器啊？

这是用"哪"的反问句，用肯定形式表示否定的意思。

This is a rhetorical question with "哪", used to indicate negation by an affirmative form.

例如：我不信，哪有这样的好事呀？

6. 除了有你知道的撞击、打破东西以外，还有失败的意思。

"除了……以外，还……"表示在什么之外还有别的。

"除了……以外，还……" means "there is something else", equivalent to "besides", "apart from" or "in addition to" in English.

例如：这次学校开运动会，我除了参加游泳比赛以外，还参加了田径比赛。

7. 那他们就可以一边劳动，一边自娱自乐了。

"一边……一边……"这一结构表示两种动作同时进行。

The structure "一边……一边……" is used to indicate that two actions are going on at the same time.

例如：他们一边学习一边工作。

替换练习 Substitution Drills

1. 别说这点儿 小事儿，	再	难	的	事	他都 能解决。
钱		多		钱	会帮助你
路		远		路	不怕
雨		大		雨	不在乎

2. 这	还真有	创意。
他		办法
你		福气
北京		不少小吃

3. 他们	可以一边	劳动，	一边	自娱自乐。
我们		工作		学习
游人		划船		欣赏风景
大家		喝咖啡		聊天儿

会话 Conversations

完成下列对话 Complete the following dialogues
(如括号里有词语或提示，请按要求做 Use the words or phrases given in the brackets)

A: 这里的海浪不大，我能游到小岛去。

B: 你不怕这海浪？

A: ______________________。(别说……就是……)

B: 祝福你顺利游到小岛。

A: 你们报名参加爬山比赛了吗？

B: 我们两个都报名了。

A: 你们班还有别人报名吗？

B: ____________________。(除了……还……)

民俗村
【第四集】

场景 Scene　摩梭族民居前

大　牛：韩佳，你这身上戴的是什么啊？

韩　佳：这是荷包啊！

大　牛：那么小的包，能装什么啊！①

韩　佳：这跟我们平时用的包可不一样，这荷包是女孩子一针一针绣出来的，戴在身上是吉祥的象征。

大　牛：原来是女孩子戴的小玩意儿，怪不得那么小。②

韩　佳：这男孩子也可以戴啊！女孩子要是遇上心上人，就会把荷包送给他。③这小小的荷包里可装着浓浓的爱情呢！

大　牛：爱情啊？我也想戴一个。

韩　佳：这民俗村里面有各种各样的婚俗，我们去看看！没准啊，你还真能戴上一个！

大　牛：那咱们就别磨蹭了，快走吧！

Zánmen bié móceng le，kuài zǒu ba!

咱们 别 磨蹭 了，快 走 吧！

Let's not waste time and get going.

Daniel: Han Jia. What's it?

Han Jia: It's "hebao".

Daniel: What can such a small bag be filled with?

Han Jia: It's different from other bags. "Hebao" is embroidered by girls stitch by stitch. It's a symbol of good luck.

Daniel: I see. It's a trinket of girls, no wonder it's so small.

Han Jia: Boys can wear it, too. Once a girl meets her beloved, she will send a "hebao" to him. The small "hebao" is filled with deep love.

Daniel: Deep love? I'd like to have one.

Han Jia: The Folk Culture Villages have various marital customs. Let's go and take a look. Maybe you can get one.

Daniel: Then stop dawdling. Let's go.

场景 Scene　摩梭族民居

韩　佳：大牛，你知道什么是母系社会吗？

大　牛：这母系社会是原始社会的一个阶段，是女性当家做主这么一种社会。

韩　佳：意思差不多，就是孩子跟着母亲姓。

大　牛：现在都是跟父亲姓的，东西方都一样。你说的这个母系社会离我们现在太遥远了。

韩　佳：但是在中国云南省，有个叫泸沽湖的地方，那里有一群人，仍然过着母系社会的生活④。

大　牛：他们是什么人？这么奇特啊？

韩　佳：摩梭人。

Han Jia: Daniel, do you know matrilineal society?

Daniel: Matrilineal society is a period in the primitive society when females played the role of decision-making.

Han Jia: Pretty close. Children followed the surnames of mothers.

Daniel: But now, they follow fathers'. It's the same in both the East and the West. Matrilineal society is too far from us.

Han Jia: But in China's Yunnan Province, there is a place called Lugu Lake where there is a group of people still leading a life of matrilineal society.

Daniel: What kind of people are they?

Han Jia: Mosuo people.

场景 Scene 摩梭族民居

韩　佳：摩梭人有走婚的习俗。

大　牛：走婚？

韩　佳：相爱的男女只有夜晚才同住在女方家中。天一亮，男方就要回到自己的家。⑤

大　牛：那他们不住在一起啊？将来有了小孩谁来养啊？

韩　佳：舅舅养啊！舅舅是一个家庭中的支柱。他不用养活自己的孩子，只养活外甥、外甥女就行了。

大　牛：简直是非常太神奇了！

韩　佳：瞧把你给急的，连话都不会说了。“非常”和“太”是两个表示程度的副词，不能同时用在形容词前面。你要么说“非常神奇”，要么说“太神奇”，不能两个一块儿用。⑥

Nǐ yàome shuō “fēicháng shénqí”, yàome shuō “tài shénqí le”.

你 要么 说 “非常 神奇”，要么 说 “太 神奇 了”。

You could say either “feichang shenqi “ or “tai shenqi le.”

Han Jia: They have a custom of "zou hun".

Daniel: "Zou hun"?

Han Jia: Men and women in love can only sleep in the women's house at night. At dawn, the men have to go back to their own houses.

Daniel: They don't live together, then who will raise their children?

Han Jia: The uncles do. Uncle is the pillar of a family. He doesn't have to raise his own children, but his nephews and nieces.

Daniel: That's amazing!

Han Jia: You are too anxious to speak. "Feichang" and "tai" are two adverbs of degree that cannot be used before an adjective at the same time. You can say "feichang shenqi" or "tai shenqi" but not the two together.

场景 Scene 绣球会

韩　佳：您好，请问……

大　牛：你是找我吗？

韩　佳：你怎么跑到这儿来了？还打扮成这个样子！

大　牛：韩佳，你先别急，听我给你解释嘛！你们中国的电视剧里不是经常有这样的一个镜头吗：一个人中了状元，穿红袍、骑大马，来到了一位姑娘的绣楼下。

韩　佳：然后这位美丽的姑娘就抛下一个绣球，砸到你身上，你还娶了那位姑娘，是不是呀？

大　牛：不是啊，你别把我放进去！我的意思是这样，我是说这里的景色太美了，就像电视剧里拍的一样，所以我就过来感受一下。

韩　佳：那状元先生，你也感受够了吧？我这老仰着头跟你说话，脖子都酸了。

大　牛：不好意思。

韩　佳：大牛，你刚才提到了状元，那你知道这状元指的是什么人啊？

大　牛：当然知道了，就是中国古代科举的第一名。

韩　佳：不简单。那你知道第二名、第三名又分别叫什么呢？

大　牛：那就是亚军和季军呗！

韩　佳：你以为在开奥运会哪？这第二名叫榜眼，第三名就叫探花。大牛，那边好像有彝族人在结婚。

Nàbiān hǎoxiàng yǒu Yízúrén zài jiéhūn.

那边 好像 有 彝族人 在 结婚。

A Yi ethnic wedding is taking place over there.

Han Jia: Hello! Excuse me.

Daniel: Are you looking for me?

Han Jia: Why did you come here and dress like this?

Daniel: Han Jia, don't worry. Listen to me. Chinese TV plays often have such a scene: A "zhuangyuan" dressed in red gown and riding a horse would come to a girl's balcony ...

Han Jia: Then the beautiful girl threw a ball made of strips of silk on you and you married her. Is it right?

Daniel: No. Don't put me in the scene. I mean the scenery here is so beautiful as if in a TV play. So I came here to experience.

Han Jia: Mr. "Zhuangyuan", have you got enough experience? I keep looking up at you and my neck is aching.

Daniel: Sorry.

Han Jia: Daniel. You mentioned "zhuangyuan" just now. Do you know what "zhuangyuan" means?

Daniel: Of course, I know. "Zhuangyuan" is the Number One Scholar who passed the imperial examinations in ancient China.

Han Jia: That's right. Do you know what the Number Two and Number Three are called?

Daniel: "Yajun" and "jijun".

Han Jia: Do you think it's Olympics? The Number Two is called "bangyan". The Number Three is "tanhua". Daniel. It seems to be a wedding of Yi people over there. Let's go and have a look.

场景 Scene 彝族歌舞

韩　佳：这个大牛又跑哪儿去了？该不是想当新郎倌找阿诗玛去了吧？

场景 Scene 彝族民居

韩　佳：大牛，你别在这儿等了，阿诗玛已经被阿黑哥娶回家了。

大　牛：她已经被娶走了？完了。

韩　佳：怎么？你还想“洞房花烛夜，金榜题名时”全都占了呀？

大　牛：人生这两件大喜事，我当然想尝试尝试了。虽然今天没有成亲，可是，你们看！

韩　佳：荷包？哪儿来的呀？我怎么没看见？

大　牛：怎么样？不错吧？该说咱们的口号了吧？

合：学说中国话，朋友遍天下！

商　贩：我的荷包一块钱可不卖。

大　牛：对不起，再见！

商　贩：我的钱呢？

韩　佳：这个大牛。

Han Jia: Where is Daniel? Does he want to be a bridegroom and is looking for Ashima?

Han Jia: Daniel. Stop waiting. Ashima has married Aheige.

Daniel: She has married. All up.

Han Jia: Why? Do you want to have both "dongfang huazhu ye" and "jinbang timing shi"?

Daniel: Of course I'd like to experience the two happiest events in life. Though I didn't marry today, but look!

Han Jia: "Hebao"? Where did you get it? I didn't see it.

Daniel: How about it? Isn't it beautiful? It's time to say our slogan:

Together: Learn Chinese and make friends everywhere.

The peddler: I won't sell my "hebao" for 1 yuan.

Daniel: Sorry. Bye-bye!

The peddler: Where's my money?

Han Jia: This Daniel.

生词 New Words and Expressions

1. 戴	（动）	dài	to wear, put on
2. 象征	（名、动）	xiàngzhēng	symbol; to symbolize
3. 磨蹭	（动）	móceng	to dawdle, loiter
4. 遥远	（形）	yáoyuǎn	distant, far-off
5. 养	（动）	yǎng	to breed
6. 神奇	（形）	shénqí	magical
7. 景色	（名）	jǐngsè	scenery, scene
8. 感受	（名、动）	gǎnshòu	feel; to feel
9. 娶	（动）	qǔ	to marry (a female)
10. 尝试	（动）	chángshì	to try, attempt

注释 Notes

1. 那么小的包，能装什么啊？

“能装什么啊”，这是一个反问句，“动词＋什么”在这里表示“不可能”，全句的意思是“包太小了，不能装东西”。

“能装什么啊” is a rhetorical question. The pattern “verb+ 什么” here means “impossible”, and the sentence means the bag is too small to hold anything”.

例如：这么点钱，能买什么呀？

2. 原来是女孩子戴的小玩意儿，怪不得那么小。

“怪不得”，副词，表示明白了原因，不再觉得奇怪，前后常有表明原因的语句。

“怪不得”, an adverb, means that one feels no wonder as one understands the cause. Clauses showing the reason or cause often go with (either before or after) the expression.

例如：他在中国生活了十年，怪不得汉语说得那么好。

3. 女孩子要是遇上心上人，就会把荷包送给他。

“要是……就……”是一个假设复句，“要是”提出一种假设，“就”引出在这种情况下会出现的结果。

“要是……就……” is a hypothetical complex sentence.“要是” raises a hypothesis, and “就” leads to the result under this hypothesis.

例如：你要是有不明白的地方就来问我。

有介词“把”的动词谓语句称为“把”字句，表示对某人、某事物施加某种动作，并强调对某人、某事物产生某种结果或影响。基本句式为：

The preposition “把” structure expresses the idea that something is imposed upon a person or a thing with a certain effect. Its basic pattern is:

主语——介词“把”——宾语——谓语动词——其他成分

Subject------	把 ------------	Object----	Predicate verb-----------	Other elements
她	把	荷包	送	给他了。
我	把	事情	办	完了。

使用“把”字句一定要注意：

Attention must be paid to:

①主语一定是动作的发出者；

The subject must be the doer of the action.

②谓语动词是及物的，并能在意义上支配、影响宾语；

The verb should be a transitive one, which can affect and control the object in meaning.

③谓语动词后必须有其他成分，可以是动词重叠式、动补结构或“了”“着”“过”；

There should be other elements following the verb, and they can be repetition of the verb, a verb-complement structure or the structure of “verb+ 了，着，过”.

④宾语是确指的；

The object must be definite.

⑤助动词或否定副词要放在介词“把”之前。

Auxiliaries or negative adverbs must be put in front of the preposition “把”.

例如：他没把书还给图书馆。

他能把事情办好吗？

4．那里有一群人，仍然过着母系社会的生活。

“着”，动态助词，表示一个动作或动作结果的状态正在持续。基本句式为：

"着"is a dynamic auxiliary word, used to express continuation of an action or state. Its basic pattern is as follows:

主语——谓语动词———着——宾语

Subject---Predicate verb---- 着 -----Object

他们　　　过　　　着　　母系社会的生活。

大家　都　　坐　　　着。

否定式是在动词前加"没（有)"。

"没（有)" is added in front of the verb to form negation.

例如：不买了，我今天没带着钱。

5．天一亮，男方就要回到自己的家。

"一……就……"这一结构表示一种动作或情况出现后，紧接着发生另一种动作或情况。可以共用一个主语，也可以分属两个主语。

The structure "一……就……" indicates a situation in which one action immediately follows another. Both actions can share the same subject and can also have two different subjects.

例如：这孩子不爱学习，一有时间就出去玩儿。
　　　他一说大家就笑了。

6．你要么说"非常神奇"，要么说"太神奇"，不能两个一块儿用。

"要么……要么……"这一结构表示两者之间只能选择其中的一个。

例如：今天晚上我们要么去看电影，要么去看足球比赛。

The structure "要么……要么……" means that only one option can be choosed between the two, similar to "either ... or ..." in English.

替换练习 Substitution Drills

1. 咱们	别	磨蹭	了，快	走	吧。
孩子们		说话		睡觉	
我们		休息		爬山	
你们		闹		学习	

2. 你	要么	说	“非常神奇”，	要么	说	“太神奇了”。
我们		去	爬山		去	游泳
大家		吃	烤鸭		吃	涮羊肉
公司		经营	家具		经营	办公用品

3. 那边	好像有	彝族人	在	结婚。
里面		人		玩电脑
树林里		小鸟		叫
河边		老人		钓鱼

会话 Conversations

完成下列对话 Complete the following dialogues
（如括号里有词语或提示，请按要求做 Use the words or phrases given in the brackets）

A: 你知道张明这两天为什么那么高兴吗？
B: 不知道，有什么好事？
A: 他考上名牌大学了。
B: 原来是这样啊！______。（怪不得）

A: 暑假的旅行计划今天晚上必须定下来了，怎么办？
B: 晚上我们两个人商量一下吧。______。（要么……要么……）
A: 还是我去找你吧。
B: 好，我在家等你。

民俗村
【第五集】

场景 Scene 锦绣中华微缩景区

大　牛：韩佳，今天你带我们来的是什么地方?

韩　佳：这里是深圳的锦绣中华微缩景区。今天我能带您一天游遍中国。

大　牛：游遍全中国只要一天?那可是既能大饱眼福，又能省脚力。

Daniel: Han Jia. Where is it?

Han Jia: It's Shenzhen Splendid China Miniature Scenic Spot. I'll take you to travel whole China just in one day.

Daniel: Travel whole China in one day. Oh, we can feast eyes and save energy.

民俗村

场景 Scene 微缩九龙壁

韩　佳：大牛，认识吗？

大　牛：有点眼熟啊！我想起来了，是北京北海的九龙壁。

韩　佳：是九龙壁，不过这可不是北海的那块，而是山西大同的九龙壁。

Zhè shì Shānxī Dàtóng de Jiǔlóngbì.

这 是 山西 大同 的 九龙壁。

This is the Nine Dragon Screen of Datong, Shanxi.

韩　佳：论岁数，这九龙壁可算是老大哥了，比北海的早三百多年呢！① 你看这些龙的龙爪，这里的龙是四爪，而北海的龙是五爪。

大　牛：哦，你不说我还真没注意。

韩　佳：大牛，我有个建议。你看，这龙有四爪，咱们不如按中国版图的东、南、西、北四个方位，来找出锦绣中华的美景，你看怎么样？

大　牛：没问题。就凭我大牛的眼力和脚下的功夫……韩佳，你别走那么快呀！

Han Jia: Daniel. Do you know it?

Daniel: It looks familiar. Oh, it's the Nine-Dragon Screen in Beijing Beihai Park.

Han Jia: It is the Nine-Dragon Screen, but not the one in Beihai Park. It's the Nine-Dragon Screen of Datong, Shanxi Province.

Han Jia: It is 300 years older than the one in Beihai Park. Look at their claws. These dragons have four claws each, but those in Beihai have five claws each.

Daniel: Oh. I didn't notice that.

Han Jia: Daniel. I have a suggestion. Since the dragon has four claws, let's find out four beautiful scenes according to the four directions of Chinese territory. Do you agree?

Daniel: No problem. Trust my eyesight and footwork. Han Jia, don't walk so fast.

场景 Scene 微缩瘦西湖

韩　佳：大牛，我找到南了！

大　牛：这么快？

韩　佳：二十四桥明月夜，玉人何处教吹箫。

大　牛：韩佳，刚才你念的是什么诗呀，我怎么听不懂啊，再说这里是哪儿啊？②

韩　佳：这里是江南的瘦西湖。刚才我念的那两句诗，是唐代诗人杜牧的诗句。二十四桥就是瘦西湖当中的一景。

大　牛：你说的是“瘦”西湖啊？咱们离开杭州才这么几个月，就把西湖给饿瘦了，这是谁干的？

韩　佳：什么呀！大牛，这瘦西湖在江苏扬州，离杭州西湖还有一段距离。扬州园林妙就妙在会巧借。③它把西湖一角的景色借过来，形成了如丝带般的长湖，所以就称做瘦西湖。这个“瘦”字还概括了清、俏的特点。

大　牛：哦，原来“瘦”在这里还有这么多含义。

韩　佳：没错，扬州园林的这种含蓄表达方式是只可意会，不可言传。

Zhǐ kě yìhuì, bù kě yánchuán.

只 可 意会，不 可 言传。

Beyond literary description.

大　牛：韩佳，虽然刚才那两句唐诗我没听懂，这成语我可在行啊！“只可意会，不可言传”就是说没办法用语言表达出来。

韩　佳：大牛解释得没错。“只可意会，不可言传”就是说只能用心去体会，而没办法用语言表达出来。

大　牛：韩佳，咱们继续找吧！

韩　佳：好！

Han Jia: Daniel, I've found the South.

Daniel: So quickly.

Han Jia: In the moonlight over the 24 bridges, where is the beautiful girl playing flute?

Daniel: Han Jia. What poem did you say? I don't understand. And where is it?

Han Jia: It's Shouxi Lake in Jiangnan. The two poem lines I just said were written by Du Mu, poet of the Tang Dynasty. The 24 bridges is a scenery of Shouxi Lake.

Daniel: Shouxi Lake? We've left Hangzhou for a few months only, how could the West Lake be so thin? Who did it?

Han Jia: Nonsense! Daniel. Shouxi Lake is in Yangzhou of Jiangsu Province at a distance to the West Lake in Hangzhou. Yangzhou gardening borrowed part of the scene of the West Lake skillfully to form a long lake like a ribbon. So, it is called Shouxi Lake. "Shou" also means clear and beautiful.

Daniel: Oh. "Shou" has so many meanings here.

Han Jia: Right. The implication expression of Yangzhou gardening is beyond literary description.

Daniel: Han Jia. Though I didn't understand the Tang poem, I am expert at idioms. "Zhi ke yihui, bu ke yanchuan" means to be impossible to describe in words.

Han Jia: Daniel is correct. "Zhi ke yihui, bu ke yanchuan" means that you can only sense it by heart but can't express it with words.

Daniel: Han Jia. Let's go on.

Han Jia: OK.

场景 Scene 微缩蓬莱阁

大　牛：蓬莱阁，山东。这不是东吗？哎，韩佳，来！

韩　佳：大牛，你找的是哪儿啊？

大　牛：我找到了蓬莱阁。这也算是一处美景吧？

韩　佳：可以啊，找了一处人间仙境。

大　牛：人间仙境是像天堂一样的地方吧？

韩　佳：可以那么说。俗话说，身在蓬莱即是仙。这里不光有很多关于神仙的传说，而且还能看到海市蜃楼呢！④

Daniel: Penglai Pavilion of Shandong Province. It's the East. Hey, Han Jia. Come here.

Han Jia: Daniel. Where is it?

Daniel: It is Penglai Pavilion, a place of beauty.

Han Jia: Good! You found a fairyland on earth.

Daniel: Is it a place like paradise?

Han Jia: You can say that. There is a common saying that you are an immortal when in Penglai. There are not only numerous fairy tales but also mirages.

场景 Scene 微缩布达拉宫

大　牛：韩佳，这就是你一定要让我看的布达拉宫啊？

韩　佳：没错，西藏拉萨的布达拉宫是中国藏传佛教的圣地，是世界上海拔最高、最雄伟的宫殿。这是西藏的吐蕃王松赞干布为了迎娶唐朝的文成公主而专门修建的[5]，到现在已经成为藏族的标志性建筑了。

Tā chéngwéile Zàngzú de biāozhìxìng jiànzhù.

它 成为了 藏族 的 标志性 建筑。

It became the building which is most representative of Tibetan architecture.

大　牛：韩佳，咱们这个东、南、西都找到了，可是北呢？

韩　佳：这么快就找不着北了？不就在那儿吗？[6]

Daniel: Han Jia. Is this the Potala Palace you recommended?

Han Jia: Yes. The Potala Palace is in Lhasa of Tibet. It is the holy land of Chinese Tibetan Buddhism, and is the most magnificent palace with the highest altitude in the world. It was built by Songtsan Gambo, King of Tubo in Tibet, in particular for marriage with Princess Wencheng of the Tang Dynasty. Now, it has become a symbolic architecture of Tibetan nationality.

Daniel: Han Jia. We have found the East, South and West, but where is the North?

Han Jia: Are you lost so soon? It's over there.

场景 Scene 微缩长城

大　牛：啊，长城！这可是一个令全世界惊叹的奇迹呀！

韩　佳：没错，长城就像一条巨龙，腾越在中国北方的山脉间。它是我们中国人的骄傲，是中华民族的象征。

大　牛：韩佳，我知道你说起这长城来，三天三夜也说不完，可是我们今天节目结束的时间就要到了。

Daniel: Aha, the Great Wall. It is a wonder of the world.

Han Jia: Yes. The Great Wall jumps over the northern mountains like a huge dragon. It's the pride of Chinese people and symbol of Chinese nation.

Daniel: Han Jia. I know you have a great deal to say about the Great Wall. But we have to stop because time is up. Let's take our audience to today's Feast for the Eyes together and feast our eyes.

生词 New Words and Expressions

1.	凭	（动）	píng	to rely on, depend on
2.	再说	（连）	zàishuō	what is more...
3.	概括	（动）	gàikuò	to sum up, summarize
4.	含蓄	（形）	hánxù	implicit, reserved
5.	方式	（名）	fāngshì	way, manner
6.	意会	（动）	yìhuì	to perceive by intuition, sense
7.	言传	（动）	yánchuán	to explain in words
8.	体会	（名、动）	tǐhuì	experience or understanding; to experience
9.	标志	（名、动）	biāozhì	mark; to mark
10.	奇迹	（名）	qíjì	miracle

注释 Notes

1. 论岁数，这九龙壁可算是老大哥了，比北海的早三百多年呢！

用介词“比”的比较句是比较两个人或两种事物在性状和程度上的差别。基本句式为：

“比”, a preposition, is used in comparison between two persons or things in quality or degree. Its basic pattern is:

A———————— 比————B———— 比较的结果

A---------------------- 比 -----------B-------------Result of the comparison

这九龙壁	比	那九龙壁	早三百多年。
这个景点	比	那个景点	好。

否定式是：

Its negative form is :

A 不比 B……

例如：这个房间不比那个房间大。

2. 刚才你念的是什么诗呀，我怎么听不懂啊，再说这里是哪儿啊？

“再说”，连词，这里表示推进一层，对前面的话加以补充。

“再说”, a conjunction, is used here to mean “further more” to supplement what is said before.

例如：他最近比较忙，所以不想去了，再说他身体也不太好。

3. 扬州园林妙就妙在会巧借。

“A就A在……”这一结构用于说明“A”的原因，有强调的语气。

The structure “A就A在……” is used to indicate the cause of “A” with a bit of emphasis.

例如：这个地方好就好在没有污染。

4. 这里不光有很多关于神仙的传说，而且还能看到海市蜃楼呢！

“不光……而且……”是一个递进复句，后一分句比前一分句表示更进一层的意思。

“不光……而且……” is a progressive complex sentence, with the latter clause having further meaning than the former.

例如：他不光会打篮球，而且足球也踢得很好。

5. 这是西藏的吐蕃王松赞干布为了迎娶唐朝的文成公主而专门修建的。

在“为了……而……”这一结构中，介词“为了”说明原因或目的，连词“而”把前面的成分连接到动词上。

In the structure “为了……而……”, the preposition “为了” indicates the cause or purpose, and the conjunction “而” links the previous element with the verb after it.

例如：他为了考上一个好大学而努力了好几年。

6. 这么快就找不着北了？不就在那儿吗？

“不……吗”是一个反问句，表示“就在那儿”。

“不……吗” is a form of rhetorical question, meaning “it is just there”.

例如：王老师不就在办公室吗，你打个电话问问他。

替换练习 Substitution Drills

1. 这是	山西大同	的	九龙壁。
	山东泰山		玉皇顶
	学校		大操场
	北京		大学城

2. 只可	意会，	不可	言传。
	观赏		触摸
	自己完成		求人帮助
	小步慢跑		剧烈运动

3. 它	成为了	藏族	的	标志性建筑。
她		我们		学习榜样
宠物		人们		好朋友
老张		全国		劳动模范

会话 Conversations

完成下列对话 Complete the following dialogues
（如括号里有词语或提示，请按要求做 Use the words or phrases given in the brackets）

A: 小姐，新的汉语大词典在哪儿啊？
B: ______________。（"不……吗"，反问）
A: 谢谢。
B: 不客气。

A: 你们学校有多少学生？
B: 我们学校有一万二，你们学校呢？
A: 我们学校有一万五。
B: 你们学校 ______________。（比）

欢乐谷

【第一集】

场景 Scene　欢乐谷

大　牛：哎呀，韩佳，我一进来就觉得这里充满了欢乐气氛。

韩　佳：这里是深圳的欢乐谷，来到欢乐谷，人人都欢乐。

大　牛：欢乐谷，光听这个名字就让人觉得高兴[①]。还等什么？赶紧出发！

韩　佳：走！

Daniel: Hey, Han Jia. I felt the festive atmosphere as soon as I walked in.

Han Jia: This is Shenzhen's Happy Valley. Everyone's happy here at Happy Valley.

Daniel: Just the name alone makes me happy. What are we waiting for? Hurry up.

Han Jia: Let's go!

欢乐谷

场景 Scene 欢乐谷

大　牛：韩佳，看什么呢？

韩　佳：皮皮刚才给了我张纸条，说让我们去它家做客。

大　牛：真的？那太好了！哎呀，这儿的人真是太热情了，刚来一天就请我们吃饭。

韩　佳：但是它是有条件的，只有我们找到了三个天、三个地，才能去它家做客②。

大　牛：啊，吃饭还有条件呢？

韩　佳：这"只有……才"表示的就是条件关系，也就是说只有满足了皮皮的条件，我们才能去它家做客。

Zhǐyǒu mǎnzúle tā de tiáojiàn, wǒmen cái néng qù tā jiā zuòkè.

只有 满足了 它 的 条件，我们 才 能 去 它 家 做客。

In order to be her guests, we must meet her requirements.

大　牛：这三个天、三个地，上哪儿去找啊？

游　客：这不是大牛和韩佳吗？你们玩过那边的"完美风暴"吗？你一上去真是翻天覆地，又好玩又刺激！③ 我先走了啊！

韩　佳：谢谢啊，再见！"翻天覆地。"大牛，这不就是一个天一个地了吗？我们赶紧去试试！

大　牛：嘿，原来是这个天这个地啊，这还不好找啊？

Daniel: What are you looking at, Han Jia?

Han Jia: Pipi left me a note just now. She invited me over.

Daniel: Really? That's nice. People here are just so friendly. We've just been here a day and she's already invited us.

Han Jia: But she has a condition. We need to find three "tian" and three "di" in order to go over to her place.

Daniel: A conditional invitation?

Han Jia: "Zhiyou...cai" expresses a conditional relationship. So, we have to fulfill Pipi's condition in order to be her guests.

Daniel: Where are we going to find three "tian" and three "di"?

One tourist: Daniel and Han Jia? Have you guys been on the Perfect Storm? It's really "fan tian fu di" up there. It's really exciting. I've got to go.

Han Jia: Thanks. See you. "Fan tian fu di." Daniel, we just got a "tian" and a "di". Let's go and try it out.

Daniel: So this is what she was talking about. It's easy for us to find out .

场景 Scene 完美风暴

大　牛：天哪，还真是翻天覆地的！

韩　佳：大牛，这才一个天一个地呢，你就不行了？

大　牛：我已经被折腾得头晕眼花了，你居然还能这么清醒啊④，真是佩服佩服！

Wǒ yǐjīng tóu yūn yǎn huā le, nǐ jūrán hái néng zhème qīngxǐng.

我 已经 头 晕 眼 花 了，你 居然 还 能 这么 清醒。

I'm already dizzy, you're still so clear-headed.

韩　佳："居然"就是表示出乎意料。放在句子中表示本来不会发生的事情竟然发生了。比如说，你是一个男子汉，居然胆子还没有我这个女孩子大。

大　牛：谁说的？你先给我找一点水来，我清醒清醒就好了。

韩　佳：水呀，你看那边有的是。⑤

Daniel: Wow, it's really "fan tian fu di".

Han Jia: Daniel, you're already like this after just one "tian" and one "di".

Daniel: I'm already totally dizzy. But you're still so clear-headed. I really envy you.

Han Jia: "Juran" expresses a surprise. In a sentence, it means something unexpected happened. For example, you're a guy, "juran" you get scared more easily than a girl like me.

Daniel: That's not true! Can you get me some water first? I need to clear my head.

Han Jia: Water? Over there ... you can have tons of it.

歡樂谷

场景 Scene 激流勇进

大　牛：这水在哪儿呢？

韩　佳：不就在那儿吗？得坐船过去，一会儿保证你就清醒了。

大　牛：韩佳，要从那么高的地方掉下来？不去不行吗？

韩　佳：你快走吧！

Daniel: Where is it?

Han Jia: Right over there. Got to ride a boat. I bet you can get your head cleared.

Daniel: Han Jia? Falling all this way down... Do I have to go?

Han Jia: Just go.

场景 Scene 激流勇进前

韩　佳：大牛，清醒了吗？

大　牛：能不清醒吗，都成落汤鸡了。⑥

韩　佳：你还行啊，学过的词都能用上。

大　牛：不过，这“激流勇进”还真是挺好玩儿的。

韩　佳：是不是有一种上天入地的感觉？

大　牛：啊，上天入地？这不是又找到了一个“天”一个“地”了吗？

韩　佳：对啊，所以我们再找一个“天”一个“地”就可以大功告成了。

dà gōng gào chéng

大　功　告　成

to complete successfully

韩　佳：“大功告成”就是说宣告任务完成了。

大　牛：“大功告成”是一个成语，就是说宣告任务完成了。“大功告成。”那我们继续找吧！

韩　佳：胆子越来越大了。⑦

Han Jia: Feel better, Daniel?

Daniel: How can I not? I'm a "luotangji".

Han Jia: Not bad use of the vocabulary you've learned.

Daniel: This Water Surge is a fun ride though.

Han Jia: Do you feel like "shang tian ru di"?

Daniel: "Shang tian ru di"? Another "tian" and "di".

Han Jia: Exactly! So, we just need to find one more to accomplish the mission.

Han Jia: "Da gong gao cheng" declares the completion of a task.

Daniel: "Da gong gao cheng" is a Chinese idiom which means to complete the task. Let's keep going.

Han Jia: You're getting better at this.

场景 Scene 天旋地转

大　牛：韩佳，上来啊！

韩　佳：不！

大　牛：上来吧，没事的！

韩　佳：不！

大　牛：有这么害怕吗？韩佳说这个叫“天旋地转”，让我来尝试一下，可是她自己先溜了。我大牛，男子汉大丈夫，怕什么呀！祝我好运吧！来，开始了！

场景 Scene 天旋地转

大　牛：这韩佳可真是把我给害苦了。我现在是心跳加速、眼冒金星，也不知道她跑哪儿去了，我得找她算账。

Daniel: Come here, Han Jia.

Han Jia: No.

Daniel: Come up, it's okay.

Han Jia: No.

Daniel: It's not that bad. Han Jia said this is "tian xuan di zhuan". I'm going to try it out. But she's already gone. Daniel, I'm a man... I'm scared of nothing! Wish me good luck! Let's get started!

Daniel: Han Jia really made me pay this time. My heart's beating fast, and my eyes are spinning. I wonder where she's gone . She'll have to pay for this.

场景 Scene 石龟群雕

大　牛：天都要黑了，这韩佳也没影儿，跑哪儿去了？算了，我还是去看看欢乐水世界的表演吧！哎，那不是韩佳吗？韩佳，我跟你说呀，这“天旋地转”，你可把我给害苦了。

场景 Scene 欢乐谷

韩　佳：据说夜幕降临的时候，在这湖面上会有一场海洋生物的盛会，待会儿我一定要看一看。

Daniel: It's getting dark. And Han Jia's gone. Where is she? Never mind. I'll just go and watch the show at happy water world. Isn't that Han Jia? Han Jia, let me tell you. " Tian xuan di zhuan" really did it to me.

Han Jia: I heard that at dusk, there will be a gathering of sea animals at the lake. I'm going to go and check it out.

生词 New Words and Expressions

1.	气氛	（名）	qìfēn	atmosphere
2.	满足	（动、形）	mǎnzú	to satisfy; satisfied
3.	条件	（名）	tiáojiàn	condition
4.	完美	（形）	wánměi	perfect
5.	居然	（副）	jūrán	unexpectedly
6.	头晕眼花		tóu yūn yǎn huā	dizzy
7.	清醒	（动、形）	qīngxǐng	to keep a cool head; cool-headed
8.	竟然	（副）	jìngrán	to one's surprise
9.	算账	（动）	suànzhàng	to settle the accounts

注释 Notes

1. 光听这个名字就让人觉得高兴。

在这个句子中，"光听这个名字"是主语，谓语部分有两个结构："让人"和"觉得高兴"。前一个动词的宾语"人"同时又是后一个动词结构"觉得高兴"的主语，这种句子称为兼语句。兼语句中第一个动词常常是"请""叫""让"等。

In this sentence, "光听这个名字" is the subject, and "让人" and "觉得高兴" are the predicate. The object "人" of the first verb "让" also is the subject of the second verb structure "觉得高兴". This kind of sentence is called pivotal sentence. In such sentences, "请" "叫" or "让" often serves as the first verb.

例如：他想请我们吃饭。
他让我们去他家做客。
这件事真叫人高兴。

2. 只有我们找到了三个天、三个地，才能去它家做客。

"只有……才……"是一个条件复句，"只有"提出实现结果的唯一条件，"才"引出上述条件产生的结果。

"只有……才……" is a conditional complex sentence, in which "只有" raises the only condition, and "才" leads to the result under such a condition.

例如：只有学好了汉语才能更好地了解中国。

3．你一上去真是翻天覆地，又好玩又刺激！

“又……又……”这一结构在这里表示同时具有两种状态。

The structure “又……又……” here indicates two states are available at the same time.

例如：这种水果又好吃又便宜，多买一些吧。

4．你居然还能这么清醒啊！

“居然”，副词，表示出乎意料。

“居然”，an adverb, means “contrary to one's expectation.

例如：我没有想到，他居然会做出这样的事。

5．水呀，你看那边有的是。

“有的是”在这里表示数量很多。

“有的是” means “a large amount”.

例如：你需要多少人帮忙，我们这里人有的是。

6．能不清醒吗，都成落汤鸡了。

“能不清醒吗”是一个反问句，强调肯定的意思。

“能不清醒吗” is a rhetorical question, emphasizing affirmation.

例如：时间这么晚了还不回来，我能不着急吗？

7．胆子越来越大了。

“越来越……”这一结构表示程度随时间的推移而增加。

The structure “越来越……” indicates the degree increases with the passing of time.

例如：夏天快要到了，天气越来越热了。

替换练习 Substitution Drills

1. 只有	满足	了	它	的	条件，	我们	才能	去它家做客。
	同意		他		要求	你们		进去参观
	兑现		你		承诺	大家		相信你
	遵守		我们		合同	我们		继续合作

2. 我	已经	头晕眼花	了，	你	居然还能这么	清醒。
他		坐立不安		你		镇静
公司		破产倒闭		他		不在乎
大家		完全绝望		他		乐观

会话 Conversations

完成下列对话　Complete the following dialogues
（如括号里有词语或提示，请按要求做　Use the words or phrases given in the brackets）

A: 汉字真难啊，怎么办？
B: ________________。（只有……才……）
A: 我每天都要花一个小时练习呀！
B: 练的时候你还要注意笔画、笔顺。

A: 今天的菜好吃吗？
B: 不错，贵吗？
A: 也不贵。
B: 这儿的菜__________，我以后也来这儿吃饭。（又……又……）

欢乐谷

【第二集】

场景 Scene 童话王国

韩　佳：我是快乐的韩佳姐姐，这位是快乐的大牛叔叔。

大　牛：怎么到这里，我就变成大牛叔叔了？韩佳，你怎么像是在主持少儿节目似的？

韩　佳：你不觉得这里像个童话王国吗？今天我们要到皮皮家去做客，可是总不能空着手去吧①？

大　牛：你的意思是……

韩　佳：我的意思是我们得带礼物去啊！

大　牛：啊？还要带礼物去啊？

韩　佳：那当然了，我们中国是礼仪之邦，最讲究礼节了，到别人家去做客，当然要带礼物了。

大　牛：还有这么多讲究，那我们带什么礼物去好呢？

韩　佳：是啊，带什么礼物去好呢？

Wǒmen dài shénme lǐwù qù ne?

我们 带 什么 礼物 去 呢？

What gifts should we bring?

小朋友：韩佳姐姐，大牛叔叔，我知道一个地方，你们跟我来好吗？

韩　佳：好啊，那我们走吧！

大　牛：大牛叔叔？我有这么老吗？

Han Jia: I'm Happy Sister Han Jia. This is Happy Uncle Daniel.

Daniel: How come I became an uncle? Han Jia, it's as if you're hosting a kids' show.

Han Jia: Don't you feel like we're in a fairy-tale world? Today, we're going to Pipi's place. We shouldn't go empty-handed.

Daniel: You mean...

Han Jia: I mean we should bring a present.

Daniel: We have to bring a present?

Han Jia: Most definitely. China is a land of courtesy and propriety. We must be polite. We must bring presents when visiting someone.

Daniel: There are so many rules. What present should we bring?

Han Jia: Yeah, what should we bring ...

A child: Sister Han Jia, Uncle Daniel. I know a good place, come with me.

Han Jia: Okay, let's go.

Daniel: Uncle Daniel? Do I really look that old?

场景 Scene 做陶艺

韩　佳：今天我要做一件礼物送给皮皮。大牛，大牛呢？怎么又不见了？再画上点儿图案以后就更锦上添花了。这可是我第一次做陶艺，我对我的这件作品还是很满意的。您看看，觉得怎么样？

Wǒ duì zìjǐ de zhè jiàn zuòpǐn hái shì hěn mǎnyì de.

我对自己的这件作品还是很满意的。

I'm very happy with this piece of work.

场景 Scene 卡通剧场

大　牛：刚才看的魔术可太有意思了，我一定要学会，待会儿到了皮皮家表演给大家看。这不是又省钱又有面子的好礼物吗？各种魔术，包教包会。真不错！

Han Jia: I'm going to make Pipi a present today, Daniel. Daniel? Where's Daniel? I just need to add some patterns and it will be all ready. It's the first time I've made pottery. I'm pretty happy with this piece of work. What do you think?

Daniel: The magic show was so interesting. I really want to learn it. I'll perform at Pipi's place for everybody.This present is fun and very economical! Teaching all kinds of magic tricks! Great!

场景 Scene 皮皮农庄前

大　牛：怎么教魔术还要钱呢？幸亏我大牛的砍价本领是一流的。[2]
韩　佳：大牛，你上哪儿去了？把什么东西藏起来了？[3]还怕我看见啊？
大　牛：没什么，没什么！韩佳，你的礼物做好了？
韩　佳：做好了，你看漂亮吗？
大　牛：除了边不够圆，颜色有点暗之外，其他都挺好的。[4]
韩　佳：你这是在夸我吗？行了，别净说我了。你的礼物准备得怎么样了？
大　牛：小小一件礼物还难得住我大牛吗？[5]不过，先不能告诉你，待会儿演给你看看。
韩　佳：说漏嘴了吧？你要表演什么节目啊？
大　牛：一会儿你就知道了。走，我们进去看看吧，我都饿了。

Daniel: I have to pay to learn? Good thing I'm a top-notch bargainer.

Han Jia: Where have you been, Daniel? What are you hiding there? Hiding from me?

Daniel: Nothing ...nothing ... Han Jia, is your present ready?

Han Jia: Yes, it is. Look, isn't it pretty?

Daniel: Except the uneven edges and the dull colors, it looks really good.

Han Jia: Is that a compliment? Never mind my present. What about yours?

Daniel: How could a little thing like this stop me? However, I couldn't tell you yet. Just wait for my performance.

Han Jia: You just said it ... What kind of performance?

Daniel: You'll find out soon. Come on, let's go inside. I'm starved.

场景 Scene 屋里

韩　佳：咦，怎么没人？大牛，快下来！

大　牛：哎，来了……

韩　佳：大牛，快过来，你看！

大　牛：哦，我明白了，原来今天就是皮皮的生日，怪不得它邀请我们过来呢！

Yuánlái jīntiān shì tā de shēngrì, guàibùde tā yāoqǐng wǒmen lái ne!

原来 今天 是 它的 生日，怪不得 它 邀请 我们 来呢！

It's her birthday today, no wonder she invited us over.

韩　佳：你刚才说的那个句子，前半句是表示原因，后半句“怪不得”是表示结果。

大　牛：又是一个因果句。

韩　佳：哎，大牛，你看，它们在叫我们呢⑥！

合：走！

Han Jia: How come no one's here? Come on down, Daniel.

Daniel: Here we go ...

Han Jia: Look over here, Daniel.

Daniel: Ah, I get it. It's Pipi' s birthday today. No wonder she invited us over.

Han Jia: In the sentence you just used, the first half expresses the cause and the second half is the result.

Daniel: Another cause-effect sentence.

Han Jia: Daniel, they're calling us over.

Together: Let's go.

场景 Scene 屋里

合：大家好，大家好！

大　牛：皮皮，我们又见面了。祝你生日快乐！

韩　佳：皮皮生日快乐！我们还给你准备了礼物呢。你看，这个是我亲手为你做的陶艺小杯子，喜欢吗？给你！

大　牛：该我了。皮皮，你看好了……这是我给你准备的生日礼物。这里有四个铁环，我们要把它们连接起来，一，二，三！再把这两个连接起来。一，二，三！一，二，三！走啊，来呀，去呀……怎么给一半的钱，还真就教我一半啊？

韩　佳：来，我们给皮皮过生日吧！

场景 Scene 庆祝生日

合：祝你生日快乐……

魔术师：瞧他们开心得连正事都忘了。⑦ 朋友们，别忘了，学说中国话，朋友遍天下！

Together: Hello, everybody!

Daniel: Pipi, we meet again! Happy birthday to you!

Han Jia: Happy birthday, Pipi! We've brought you presents. Look, a pottery mug I made just for you. Do you like it? It's for you.

Daniel: My turn. Watch carefully, Pipi ... This is my birthday present to you. We have four rings here. I'm going to connect all of them. One ... two ... three! Now, these two here ... One ... two ... three! One ... two ... three! Come and go ... Come and go ... He only taught me half of it because I only paid half price!

Han Jia: Come on, let's celebrate!

Together: Happy birthday to you ...

The Magician: Look, how happy they are. They even forgot their work. Friends, don't forget: Learn Chinese and make friends everywhere.

生词 New Words and Expressions

1．礼物	（名）	lǐwù	gift, present
2．讲究	（动、形）	jiǎngjiu	to be particular about; exquisite
3．作品	（名）	zuòpǐn	works
4．满意	（动）	mǎnyì	to be satisfied with
5．幸亏	（副）	xìngkuī	fortunately
6．藏	（动）	cáng	to hide
7．夸	（动）	kuā	to praise
8．邀请	（动）	yāoqǐng	to invite
9．亲手	（副）	qīnshǒu	by one's own hand
10．连接	（动）	liánjiē	to link, connect

注释 Notes

1．可是总不能空着手去吧？

"总"，副词，在这里表示无论怎么样一定如此。

"总"，an adverb, means "it must be so whatever happens".

例如：事实总是事实，你不能去否认它。

"空着手"在这里做状语，表示"去"的方式。

"空着手" here serves as an adverbial, indicating the manner of "去".

例如：老师站着上课。

2．幸亏我大牛的砍价本领是一流的。

"幸亏"，副词，表示由于某种有利的条件而侥幸避免了不良的后果，一般用在主语前。

"幸亏"，an adverb, indicates that undesirable results are avoided due to a certain favorable condition, and it is usually put before the subject.

例如：幸亏你提醒我，要不我就忘了。

3．把什么东西藏起来了？

"起来"用在动词后表示动作完成并达到目的。

"起来" used after a verb indicates the completion of an action and the attainment of the aim .

例如：上星期学校的足球俱乐部建立起来了。

4．除了边不够圆，颜色有点暗之外，其他都挺好的。

"除了……（之外）…… 都……"这一结构表示排除特殊，强调一致。

The structure "除了……（之外）……都……" excludes the exceptions and emphasizes the accordance.

例如：我们班除了我以外，别的人都喜欢看足球比赛。

5．小小一件礼物还难得住我大牛吗？

这是用副词"还"的反问句，意思是"难不住我大牛"。

This is a rhetorical question with "还", meaning "难不住我大牛"(it can't beat me Daniel).

例如：下雨了，还不快进来。

6．它们在叫我们呢！

副词"在"或"正在"用在动词或动词词组前，句尾加语气助词"呢"，表示一个动作正在进行。基本句式为：

Adverb "在" or "正在" is used before a verb or verb phrase, and the modal particle "呢" is added at the end of the sentence. It is used to indicate that an action is going on. Its basic pattern is:

主语——	在（正在）——	谓语动词——	宾语——	呢
Subject------	在（正在)------	Predicate verb ------	Object------	呢
他	在	玩儿	游戏	呢！
我们	正在	开	会	呢！

否定式用"没有／在……"。

The negative form is "没有／在……".

例如：他没在睡觉，他在看书呢！

7．瞧他们开心得连正事都忘了。

"连……都（也）……"这一结构用于表示强调。

The structure "连……都（也）……" is used for emphasis.

例如：为了赶九点的飞机，他连饭都没吃就走了。

替换练习 Substitution Drills

1. 我们	带	什么	礼物	去呢？
	拿		东西	
	送		鲜花	
	开		汽车	

2. 我	对自己的	这件作品	还是很	满意	的。
他		那张油画		珍惜	
她		这个女儿		喜欢	
我们		这些成就		自豪	

3. 原来	今天	是	它	的	生日，怪不得	它邀请我们来	呢！
	这里		你		故乡	你这么了解情况	
	北京		中国		古都	它有那么多名胜古迹	
	她		他		妈妈	她特别关心他	

会话 Conversations

完成下列对话　Complete the following dialogues
（如括号里有词语或提示，请按要求做　Use the words or phrases given in the brackets）

A: 昨天晚上你睡得太晚了吧？
B: 我一点多才睡。
A: 今天早上我要不叫你，你还得睡。
B: 是。________________，要不我上课又得迟到了。（幸亏）

A: 这件衬衫多少钱？
B: 十五块。
A: 太贵了。
B: ________________，别的地方都卖二十块。（用“还”反问）

欢乐谷
【第三集】

场景 Scene 欢乐谷

韩　佳：哎，大牛我还没发现，今天怎么这身打扮啊？

大　牛：怎么样，够帅的吧[①]？像不像英俊的西部牛仔？

韩　佳：这帽子还真不错。那你为什么要打扮成西部牛仔的样子？而且还背着一个大包啊？

大　牛：今天我要淘金去。

韩　佳：淘金？你没事吧？这儿是欢乐谷，哪来的金可淘啊？

大　牛：一看就知道你没有好好看地图啊！你看，这片都是金矿镇，这镇子里能没有金矿吗？

韩　佳：真是个财迷！好了，那今天就陪大牛去逛逛金矿镇，我要看你到底能找出什么宝贝来[②]。

大　牛：好，出发吧！

韩　佳：走！

Wǒ yào kàn nǐ dàodǐ néng zhǎo chū shénme bǎobèi lai.

我要看你到底能找出什么宝贝来。

I'd like to see what treasures you can find.

Han Jia: Hey, I just noticed that you're all dressed up today.

Daniel: What do you think? Do I look like a handsome cowboy?

Han Jia: The hat's pretty nice. Why are you dressed up like a cowboy? And what's with the bag?

Daniel: Today, I'm going to dig for gold.

Han Jia: Are you alright? There's no gold here in Happy Valley.

Daniel: I know at the first hint that you don't look at the map carefully. All this area is Gold Mine Town. The town must have gold mines.

Han Jia: Your mind's never off money. Okay. I'll go to Gold Mine Town with you today. I'm going to see what you will come up with.

Daniel: Okay, let's go!

Han Jia: Let's go.

场景 Scene 金矿镇

韩　佳：哇，这里真的就像电影中的西部小镇一样。

大　牛：这里是金矿的故乡，也是我梦中的地方。

韩　佳：他怎么连做梦都在想金子！

大　牛：韩佳，嘟哝什么呢？你看我这个，怎么样？

韩　佳：太帅了，简直是英姿勃发，高大挺拔！③

大　牛：你是在说我吧？

韩　佳：我是在说它。

大　牛：啊？

Han Jia: This is just like a Western town in the movies.

Daniel: This is home of gold mines. And home of my dreams!

Han Jia: He even dreams about gold!

Daniel: What are you mumbling about? Look at this, what do you think?

Han Jia: Perfectly handsome. Heroic and grand!

Daniel: You're talking about me, right?

Han Jia: I'm talking about him!

Daniel: Huh?

场景 Scene 金矿镇

大　牛：哎，韩佳，等一下，这里好像是一间铁匠铺啊！反正我们没有工具，不如打一件吧！④

韩　佳：这个大牛，今天是不见金子不死心了。⑤ 算了，就随他去吧！

大　牛：走！

场景 Scene 金矿镇

大　牛：哎，韩佳，刚才你说的那个"死心"是什么意思？

Nǐ shuō de "sǐxīn" shì shénme yìsi?

你说的"死心"是什么意思？

What did you mean by "sixin"?

韩　佳："死心"就是断了念头的意思。

大　牛：我知道了。"死心"，"死"读三声，"心"读一声，就是"断了念头"的意思，"死心"。韩佳，这里怎么没人呢？哦，我知道了……一定是老板也淘金去了。

韩　佳：你以为谁都跟你一样啊？⑥ 那现在怎么办呢？

大　牛：只好自己动手。韩佳，你看我的吧！

Daniel: Wait here, Han Jia. There's a blacksmith's shop. I'm getting some tools since I didn't bring any.

Han Jia: Daniel won't "sixin" without gold today. I'll just let him be.

Daniel: Let's go.

Daniel: Han Jia, you said something about "sixin". What does it mean?

Han Jia: "Sixin" means to stop thinking about something.

Daniel: I see. "Sixin", third tone, first tone, means to give up on a certain idea. "Si-xin." How come there's no one here, Han Jia? Oh, I get it ... The owner must've gone to dig gold too.

Han Jia: You think everybody's like you? Then ... what do you do now?

Daniel: Use my own hands. Just watch me, Han Jia.

场景 Scene　金矿镇

韩　佳：大牛，这儿哪有什么金矿啊？找了半天了，都累死了。

大　牛：韩佳，别泄气啊，找金子哪有那么容易啊？

韩　佳：可是我觉得这里根本就没有什么金矿。我不能再被你左右了⑦，你自己找吧！

大　牛：韩佳，等等，刚才你说了，“你被我左右了”，到底是左还是右啊？

韩　佳：不是左也不是右。这“左右”除了可以分别表示方位以外，合在一起就是一个动词，是“操纵”“支配”的意思。我们可以说：“你左右不了我的思想，更左右不了我的行动。”

Nǐ zuǒyòu bu liǎo wǒ de sī xiǎng, gèng zuǒyòu bu liǎo wǒ de xíngdòng.

你左右不了我的思想，更左右不了我的行动。

You can't control my thoughts, and you'll never control my actions.

大　牛：我终于明白了。“左”“右”可以表示方向，用在一起还有“控制”的意思。“左右。”

韩　佳：我再也不听你的支配，再也不听你的话了！我要休息会儿，不走了！你也别……大牛怎么变黑了？哎呀，洪水来了！大牛，快跑！

Han Jia: Daniel, where are the gold mines? I'm exhausted after all this search.

Daniel: Don't give up, Han Jia. Finding gold isn't that easy.

Han Jia: But I feel that there's no gold mine here at all. I can't let you control me anymore. You go on your own.

Daniel: Wait, Han Jia. You said you can't let me "zuoyou ..." Is it "zuo" or "you"?

Han Jia: It's neither. "Zuoyou", besides expressing directions, is also a verb when used together. It means to control and influence. We can say, you can't influence my thoughts, let alone control my actions.

Daniel: I finally understand. Apart from meaning left and right, "zuoyou", when used together means to control. "Zuoyou."

Han Jia: I will no longer follow your orders or listen to you. I need to rest. No more walking. Don't ... Why are you so dark? The flood is coming! Run, Daniel, run!

歡樂谷

场景 Scene 金矿镇

大　牛：一场洪水冲垮了小镇，也冲垮了我的淘金梦。

韩　佳：你呀，是该清醒清醒了。肯定是西部牛仔的故事看多了，所以才会胡思乱想。您看，咱们身后的这小镇，还不是一样充满着欢笑吗？

大　牛：没错，虽然没有找到金矿，可是我们确实感受到了这里的欢乐气氛。

韩　佳：没错！

大　牛：韩佳，这不是金子吗？哎，我大牛终于找到金子了！

韩　佳：既然你的愿望已经实现了，我们今天的节目也该结束了。一起喊出我们的口号：

合：学说中国话，朋友遍天下！

小朋友：大哥哥，请把我的巧克力还给我。

大　牛：哦，小妹妹，这是你的啊？那你拿好。我的金子啊！

Daniel: The flood destroyed the town, and destroyed my dreams.

Han Jia: You really need to sober up. You must have watched too many Westerns. That's why you're thinking all this. Look at the town behind us. It's still as happy as it ever was.

Daniel: That's right. Although we didn't find gold mines, we truly felt the happy atmosphere here today.

Han Jia: Exactly.

Daniel: Look, Han Jia, gold! I finally found gold!

Han Jia: Since your wish has come true, we should wrap up our show today. Together with our slogan:

Together: Learn Chinese and make friends everywhere!

A child: Big brother! Please give me back my chocolate!

Daniel: It's yours, little sister? Take it then ... my gold!

生词 New Words and Expressions

1. 打扮	（动）	dǎban	to dress up
2. 到底	（副）	dàodǐ	*used in questions for emphasis*
3. 宝贝	（名）	bǎobèi	treasure, darling
4. 故乡	（名）	gùxiāng	home place, hometown
5. 工具	（名）	gōngjù	tool
6. 只好	（副）	zhǐhǎo	to have to cannot bnt
7. 根本	（副、名）	gēnběn	fundamentally; foundation
8. 控制	（动）	kòngzhì	to control
9. 感受	（动、名）	gǎnshòu	to feel; experience
10. 愿望	（名）	yuànwàng	wish

注释 Notes

1. 够帅的吧？

“够”，副词，修饰形容词，表示程度很高。句尾常有“的”或“了”。

“够”，an adverb, is used to modify adjectives, indicating a high degree. “的” or “了” is often put at the end of such sentences.

例如：今天天气够冷的，别出去了。

2. 我要看你到底能找出什么宝贝来。

“到底”，副词，用于疑问句，表示进一步追究。

“到底”，an adverb, is used in a question, indicating further inquiries.

例如：你说说，事情到底怎么样了？

3. 太帅了，简直是英姿勃发，高大挺拔！

“简直”，副词，表示完全如此或差不多如此，含有夸张语气。

“简直”，an adverb, expresses the idea “perfectly so” or “nearly so”, with a bit of exaggeration.

例如：这张风景画简直像真的一样。

4. 反正我们没有工具，不如打一件吧！

"反正"，副词，这里用于说明原因。

"反正"，an adverb, is used to indicate the reason.

例如：反正路不远，我们就走着去吧。

5. 这个大牛，今天是不见金子不死心了。

"不……不……"，这是一种双重否定的结构，表示肯定的意思。

"不……不……"，a double negative structure, is used to show affirmation.

例如：今天晚上我不做完作业不睡觉。

6. 你以为谁都跟你一样啊？

"跟……一样"这一结构用于比较两个人或两件事物性状的异同。基本句式如下：

The structure "跟……一样" is used for comparison between two persons or things in quality or state. Its basic sentence pattern is :

A ———— 跟———— B ————一样

这辆车　跟　那辆车　一样。

否定式有两种：

There are two forms of negation :

"A 跟 B 不一样" 或 "A 跟 B 一样"。

例如：这本书跟那本书不一样。

这本书不跟那本书一样。

"跟……一样" 除了做谓语以外，还可以做定语或状语。

Apart from serving as the predicate, "跟……一样" can also serve as the attributive or adverbial.

例如：我也要买一件跟这件一样的毛衣。（定语）

吃中餐跟吃西餐一样贵。（状语）

7. 我不能再被你左右了。

用介词"被"来表示被动意义的动词谓语句称为"被"字句。它说明人或事物受到某种动作的影响，产生某种结果。基本句式为：

The preposition“被” structure, used in passive construction, indicates that a person or a thing is affected by a certain action and produces a certain effect. Its basic pattern is :

主语———介词“被”————宾语—— 谓语动词————其他成分。

Subject-------Preposition “被” ------Object-----Predicate verb-------Other elements

我们	被	老师	批评	了。
骨头	被	小狗	叼到	外面去了。

“被”的宾语在意义上是动作的发出者（施事者），有时可以省略。

The object of“被”is actually the doer of the action, and sometimes it can be omitted.

例如：窗户被（风）吹开了。

“被”字句中的谓语动词一定是及物的，一般是能支配或影响句中主语（受事者）的。

The predicate verb should be transitive, which can affect or control the subject (recipient) of the sentence.

例如：上课的时候，他被老师批评了。（老师批评他了。）

“被”字句的谓语动词后一定要有其他成分，一般是动态助词“了”“过”或各种补语。

After the predicate verb of the passive sentence there must be other elements, generally the dynamic auxiliary words as “了”“过” or other different complements.

否定副词或助动词要放在“被”的前面。

The negative adverb or auxiliary verb should be put before “被”.

例如：门前的小树没有被风刮倒。

你这样做一定会被人发现。

“被”也可以用“叫”“让”代替，用“叫”“让”的被动句常用于口语，而且作为施动者的宾语一定要出现。

“被” can also be replaced by “叫”“让”, which are often used in spoken Chinese and the object to the doer must appear in the sentence.

例如：衣服叫风刮跑了。

碗让妹妹打破了。

替换练习 Substitution Drills

1.	我	要看你到底能	找	出什么	宝贝	来。
	大家		做		好吃的	
	群众		调查		问题	
	他		拿		证据	

2.	你	说的	"死心"	是	什么	意思?
	他		名胜	在		地方
	你们		新发现	有		价值
	中国人		中秋节	有		讲究

3.	你	左右	不了	我	的	思想,	更	左右	不了	我	的	行动。
		控制		他		言论		控制		他		活动
		掌握		自己		现在		掌握		自己		未来
		限制		别人		行为		限制		别人		思想

会话 Conversations

完成下列对话　Complete the following dialogues
(如括号里有词语或提示,请按要求做　Use the words or phrases given in the brackets)

A: 你一会儿说去,一会儿说不去,＿＿＿＿＿＿＿＿?(到底)
B: 去,去!
A: 星期天上午九点集合,带好你的东西。
B: 没问题,我一定准时到。

A: 飞机几点起飞?
B: 下午五点半。咱们三点去机场。
A: 现在不到一点,时间还早着呢!
B: 是呀,＿＿＿＿＿＿＿＿,你慢慢收拾吧!(反正)

亚洲首座四维影院
欢乐谷
HAPPY VALLEY
PIRATES
海盗

欢乐谷
【第四集】

场景 Scene 欢乐谷造型船上

韩　佳：船长，这船要往哪儿开啊？

大　牛：哈哈，欢乐岛！

韩　佳：怎么还会说话？声音还有点熟。大牛，出来！

大　牛：韩佳，把你吓了一跳吧？

韩　佳：节目都开始了①，你还躲着干吗呀？

大　牛：快乐学汉语，轻松又好记！大家好，我是快乐的大牛！

韩　佳：我是快乐的韩佳，这里是《快乐中国》！

大　牛：韩佳，你看，我也没忘记跟观众朋友们打招呼吧！

韩　佳：大牛，你说的那个欢乐岛在哪儿啊？带我去逛逛吧！

大　牛：就是……

别　人：快上船，去欢乐岛喽！

韩　佳：哎，还有，还有，还有人哪！不用你了，我坐船去了。

大　牛：韩佳，等等我！我也不认识啊！

Han Jia: Where are we heading, Captain?

Daniel: Haha ... Happy Island!

Han Jia: He can talk? And it sounds so familiar too. Come out, Daniel!

Daniel: I startled you, Han Jia.

Han Jia: The show's started. Stop hiding yourself.

Daniel: Learn Chinese the fun way. It's easy to remember! Hello, everyone. I'm Happy Daniel.

Han Jia: And I'm Merry Han Jia. Welcome to *Happy China*.

Daniel: See, Han Jia, I didn't forget to greet our audience.

Han Jia: Where's the Happy Island, Daniel? Can you take me there?

Daniel: Well ...

Others: Let's get on the boat to Happy Island!

Han Jia: Oh, there's somebody else. Don't worry about it. I'll ride the boat over.

Daniel: Wait for me, Han Jia! I don't know the way either!

场景 Scene 极限运动营

韩　佳：这欢乐岛上可真热闹啊！

大　牛：韩佳，你看，这里是极限运动营。其实这极限运动，我大牛原来也玩过，不难！

韩　佳：那你可别光说不练。②

大　牛：这句话我知道，是歇后语，“天桥的把式，光说不练”。

Nǐ kě bié guāng shuō bú liàn.
你可别光说不练。

Don't just procrastinate.

韩　佳：歇后语倒是会说，但是这极限运动，总应该给我们露一手吧！

大　牛：现在这么多人看着我。

韩　佳：这么多人看着你，你才不能丢脸呢！③

大　牛：好，我去准备一下。准备好了！

韩　佳：这可真是“人靠衣服，牛靠打扮”。大牛穿上这一身，马上就不一样了。

大　牛：什么“人靠衣服，牛靠打扮”？明明是“人靠衣服，马靠鞍”。

韩　佳：这大牛还真蒙不住，其实我就是想说你穿上这一身以后，整个人马上就不一样了。

大　牛：“人靠衣服，马靠鞍”意思是说，穿上这身衣服，整个人马上就不一样了。好了，现在看看我大牛给你们表演，看看我是不是光说不练。

韩　佳：好，来吧！

Han Jia: It is so lively and energetic here.

Daniel: Look, Han Jia. This is the extreme sports camp. Actually, I've played extreme sports before. It's nothing.

Han Jia: Don't just talk, Daniel.

Daniel: This I know ... A two-part allegorical saying. "Tianqiao de bashi, guang shuo bu lian."

Han Jia: You know your two-part allegorical saying, but extreme sports ... Shouldn't you show us a little?

Daniel: But so many people are watching me.

Han Jia: Everybody's watching, so don't blow it!

Daniel: Okay, I'll go get ready. I'm all set.

Han Jia: "Ren kao yifu, niu kao daban." With this outfit, Daniel really looks different.

Daniel: What "ren kao yifu, niu kao daban"? It should be "ren kao yifu, ma kao an"!

Han Jia: Daniel's a smart one. I meant that you look different with this set of gear on.

Daniel: "Ren kao yifu, ma kao an" means the clothes make it the man. Okay, time for my performance. You'll see if I'm all talks.

Han Jia: OK. Come on!

场景 Scene 极限运动营

大　牛：现在看我的了，走喽……韩佳，快扶我起来！

场景 Scene 心语神泉

大　牛：我都渴了，要是有点儿水喝就好了。
韩　佳：是呀！
大　牛：怎么回事啊？
韩　佳：是啊……
大　牛：哎哟！

Yàoshi yǒu diǎn shuǐ hē jiù hǎo le.
要是 有 点 水 喝 就 好 了。

It would be nice to have some water.

大　牛：它不会和我有心灵感应吧？
韩　佳：它又不是人，怎么会有心灵感应？④ 我觉得它这里面应该有个装置，或者是声控的，或者是光控的。⑤ 你说呢？
大　牛：我觉得是人控的。
韩　佳：啊，人控？

Daniel: Just watch me ... Here I go! Help me up, Han Jia!

Daniel: I think I need some water.

Han Jia: Yeah.

Daniel: What's going on?

Han Jia: Yeah ...

Daniel: Hmm ...

Daniel: Is there some kind of telepathy between us?

Han Jia: It's not a human being ... no telepathies. I think there's some kind of a rig inside. It's controlled either by sound or by light. What do you think?

Daniel: I think it's controlled by a person.

Han Jia: A person?

歡樂谷

场景 Scene 地道战

大　牛：刚才这么近距离地看拍电影，真过瘾！

韩　佳：声音都是从现场发出来的，听着又真实又刺激。

大　牛：不过电影里有很多声音都是配的。

Diànyǐng li de hěn duō shēngyīn shì pèi shangqu de.

电影 里的 很 多 声音 是 配 上去 的。

Lots of the sounds in movies are dubbed.

韩　佳：没错，前面就有个地方可以告诉大家，电影里的声音是怎么配出来的。如果想知道，就去看看吧！⑥

Daniel: It was so fun to watch a movie production up close.

Han Jia: The sound was all produced on set. They were real and exciting.

Daniel: But a lot of movie sounds were dubbed afterwards.

Han Jia: That's right. There's a place up there that tells us how some of the movie sounds were made. Go to see it if you want to find out.

场景 Scene 香格里拉特技影视馆

大　牛：你好，请问这些都是什么东西啊？

音效师：是不是觉得有点稀奇古怪的？其实这些东西看起来挺奇怪的⑦，但是它都是电影里面配音的道具。每一个都会发出不同的声音。这个你把它转起来，你就知道了。

韩　佳：听着像寒冬里刺骨的风吹来一样，是吗？

音效师：对，刮风。声音大一点它就是大风，轻呢，那就是微风。

大　牛：挺像！那还有别的吗？

音效师：还有好几样呢！还有这个，你们试一下这个，这个比较好玩。

大　牛：试试！

韩　佳：打雷了，打雷！

音效师：对，就是打雷的声音。

大　牛：很恐怖。那有没有下雨的？

音效师：没有下雨，有别的。来，那看下一个。这个就是家用的磁带，很简单的东西，但是你要按照走路的速度，这样来捏它，它就是过草地的效果。

韩　佳：好，那我试一下。

大　牛：走得慢，跑了……

大　牛：跑步。

韩　佳：像不像？

大　牛：挺像的！

Daniel: Hello. Could you tell us about these things?

Audiosound Technician: Do they look very strange? Although these things look strange, they are all used to make sounds. Each thing produces a different sound. You'll find out if you turn that thing.

Han Jia: Sounds like howling wind in the winter. Right?

Audiosound Technician: Yes, wind. The louder the sound, the stronger the wind. Weak sound would be a breeze.

Daniel: Very nice. Anything else?

Audiosound Technician: There's a lot. Look at this. You can try this. It's really fun.

Daniel: Let's try it.

Han Jia: Hey, there goes thunder!

Audiosound Technician: Yep. The sound of thunder.

Daniel: Very horrifying. Do you have rain?

Audiosound Technician: No, but I have others. Look at this here. This is a normal cassette tape. A very simple thing. But if you squeeze it in the rhythm of walking, it'll sound like walking on grass.

Han Jia: Okay, let me try it.

Daniel: Walking slowly ... Running ...

Daniel: Running.

Han Jia: Sound real?

Daniel: Yep.

场景 Scene 欢乐岛

韩　佳：今天在这欢乐岛上玩得可真开心啊！

大　牛：今天我们也累了。韩佳，咱们还是快点回去休息吧！

Han Jia: Today was nicely spent on Happy Island.

Daniel: We're all exhausted. Han Jia, we need to go get rested.

生词 New Words and Expressions

1.	打招呼		dǎ zhāohu	to greet someone
2.	光	（副、形、名）	guāng	only; smooth; light
3.	丢脸	（动）	diūliǎn	to loose face
4.	靠	（动）	kào	to rely on
5.	蒙	（动）	mēng	to cheat, deceive
6.	配	（动）	pèi	to match
7.	过瘾	（形）	guòyǐn	full enjoyed
8.	稀奇古怪		xīqí gǔguài	queer
9.	按照	（动）	ànzhào	to follow
10.	效果	（名）	xiàoguǒ	effect

注释 Notes

1. 节目都开始了。

"都"，副词，在这里相当于"已经"的意思，句尾常有"了"。

"都"，an adverb, means "already", often used with "了" at the end of a sentence.

例如：都十二点了，还不睡觉啊？

2. 那你可别光说不练。

"可"，副词，表示强调。

"可"，an adverb, is used for emphasis.

例如：你可不能再忘了带词典了。

"光"，副词，是"只"的意思。

"光"，an adverb, means "only".

例如：这个孩子一天到晚光想玩儿，不想学习。

3. 这么多人看着你，你才不能丢脸呢！

"才"，副词，表示强调所说的事，句尾常有助词。

"才", an adverb, emphasizes what is said, often used with "呢" at the end of the sentence.

例如：这样的事我才不干呢！

4. 它又不是人，怎么会有心灵感应？

"怎么会有心灵感应"是一个反问句，用肯定的形式表示否定的意思，"怎么"在这里只表示反问语气。

"怎么会有心灵感应" is a rhetorical question, indicating negation with an affirmative form. "怎么" is used to indicate the rhetorical tone.

例如：这么难的文章，小学生怎么能看懂呢？

5. 我觉得它这里面应该有个装置，或者是声控的，或者是光控的。

"或者……或者……"这一结构表示一种选择关系。

The structure "或者……或者……" is used to indicate an alternative relationship.

例如：山上和山下都有景点，或者先看山上的，或者先看山下的，你们自己决定。

6. 如果想知道，就去看看吧。

"如果……就……"是一个假设复句，"如果"提出假设，"就"说明在这种情况下会出现的结果。

"如果……就……"is a hypothetic complex sentence. "如果" raises the hypothesis, and "就" indicates the result under such a hypothesis.

例如：这种礼物是不错，如果你喜欢就买嘛！

7. 这些东西看起来挺奇怪的。

"看起来"是插入语，表示估计。

"看起来", a parenthesis, indicates estimation.

例如：九点了，看起来他们是不会来了。

替换练习 Substitution Drills

1. 你可别光	说	不	练。		
	玩儿		睡		
	干活		休息		
	挑好的		要差的		

2. 要是有	点儿	水	喝	就好了。
	些	水果	吃	
	张	沙发	坐	
	本	书	看	

3. 电视里	的很多	声音	是	配	上去的。
沙漠中		树		种	
历史小说里面		情节		加	
长城上		砖		背	

会话 Conversations

完成下列对话　Complete the following dialogues

（如括号里有词语或提示，请按要求做　Use the words or phrases given in the brackets）

A: 好几天没看见老李了，他怎么了？

B: 他病了。

A: ________，他身体很好呀！（用“怎么”反问）

B: 最近工作太多，太累了。

A: 你给他们打电话了吗？我们哪天去？

B: 他们说 ________ 都可以。（或者……或者……）

A: 我们还是星期六去吧！

B: 行，我给他们打个电话就是了。

欢乐谷

【第五集】

场景 Scene　冒险山

合：我们是《快乐中国》队！

观　众：我们是《快乐中国》的热心观众，我们是快乐观众队！

韩　佳：今天啊，我们要在深圳欢乐谷的冒险山，举行一场别开生面的比赛——森林攀爬。

大　牛：韩佳，你刚一上来，你就说了一个成语，“别开生面”。这个成语的意思是另有创新的形式。我看，今天在我们比赛的同时，也来一个成语大比拼，怎么样？

观　众：没问题，我们是兵来将挡，水来土掩，勇夺第一！

大　牛：哦，这就开始了。

韩　佳：是啊，大牛，你看我们的快乐观众队信心多足啊，咱们也不能示弱。

大　牛：没问题，有我大牛在，我们肯定第一。

韩　佳：那就出发！

大　牛：走！

Together : We are Team Happy China.

Fans : We are fans of the program. We are Team Happy Fans.

Han Jia: Today, we are going to have a novel competition at Happy Valley's Adventure Hill.

Daniel: Han Jia, you just used an idiom at the start of the show. "Bie kai sheng mian". This idiom means creative and novel. I propose that we have an idiom competition at the same time.

Fans : No problem. We will "bing lai jiang dang, shui lai tu yan" and go for first place!

Daniel: They've already started.

Han Jia: Yeah, Daniel. Look how confident Team Happy Fans are. We must keep up.

Daniel: No problem. With me here, we're Number One for sure.

Han Jia: Then, let's go.

Daniel: Let's go!

场景 Scene 冒险岛爬绳梯

韩　佳：大牛，加油 ！

大　牛：这个太简单了。对我大牛来说就是“小试牛刀”。[①]

Zhège tài jiǎndān le, duì wǒ lái shuō shì “xiǎo shì niú dāo”.

这个太简单了，对我来说是“小试牛刀”。

This is too easy, it's just a piece of cake for me.

韩　佳：小心，你呀，就别吹牛了，抓紧时间！

观　众：加油！我这是一鼓作气！

大　牛：哎，观众朋友们，刚才听到了吗？“一鼓作气”是一个成语，意思是一口气完成一件事。“一鼓作气。”

裁　判：好，来，继续。下一位，快，那边！

Han Jia: Go, Daniel!

Daniel: This is too easy. This is " xiao shi niu dao"for me.

Han Jia: Stop bragging, be careful! Let's hurry up!

Fans: Let's go! This is "yi gu zuo qi".

Daniel: Dear friends, did you hear that? " Yi gu zuo qi" is a Chinese idiom which means to do something all in one go. " Yi gu zuo qi" .

The Judge: Okay, let's keep going! Next! Over there.

场景 Scene

冒险岛

大　牛：来，加油！

韩　佳：好了，大牛，该你了。② 刚才真是把我吓死了③，真是惊心动魄呀。"惊心动魄"就是形容非常紧张，把魂魄都给震动了。④ 大牛。

观　众："如履平地。"

韩　佳：他居然说像在平地上走一样轻松。

大　牛：韩佳，你先歇会儿，免得待会儿就没劲儿了⑤。

Nǐ xiān xiē huìr, miǎnde dāi huìr méi jìnr le.

你先歇会儿，免得待会儿没劲儿了。

Take a break now, that way you won't be exhausted in a minute.

韩　佳：这大牛，还挺会关心队友！他刚才用"免得"说了一个表示目的关系的复句，意思就是避免发生不希望发生的事情。比如说："大牛，你小心脚底下的绳子，免得摔倒了。"哎呀，他还真摔倒了⑥。

观众A：加油！

观众B：我这是快马加鞭！

Daniel: Come on!

Han Jia: Okay, Daniel, your turn. That was really scary! It was "jing xin dong po"! " Jing xin dong po" means so intense that it shakes the soul. Daniel.

Fans: " Ru lü pingdi".

Han Jia: He thinks it's like walking on level ground.

Daniel: Han Jia, take a rest here so you won't be exhausted later.

Han Jia: Daniel's being really caring. He used the term " miande", which expresses a motive relationship. It means to keep the unwanted from happening. For example, watch for that rope, so you won't trip. Oops, he really tripped.

Fans A : Play up!

Fans B : This is " kuai ma jia bian"!

场景 Scene 冒险岛

大　牛：韩佳，加油啊！
韩　佳：好！
大　牛：这比赛还不到一半，我大牛已经伤痕累累了。

场景 Scene 冒险岛

大　牛：来，韩佳，加油啊！
韩　佳：大牛，又该轮到你了。抓紧时间！

场景 Scene 冒险岛

大　牛：韩佳，快帮帮我，我的脚被卡住了！
韩　佳：大牛，你怎么变蜗牛了？该减肥了吧？这可真是进退两难啊！

Zhè kě zhēn shì jìn tuì liǎng nán a!
这可真是进退两难啊！
This really is a dilemma.

场景 Scene 冒险岛

观　众：快，坚持不懈！
韩　佳：大牛，我们要把耽误的时间赶回来！
大　牛：好，《快乐中国》队必胜！
韩　佳：我可真是单枪匹马，翻山越岭，跋山涉水呀！
观　众：我这轻而易举。走！快！
大　牛：这个我们在海南学过，他竟然说这个容易⑦！

Daniel: Go, Han Jia!

Han Jia: Okay!

Daniel: The competition's only half way through, I'm already full of cuts and bruises.

Daniel: Come on, Han Jia!

Han Jia: Your turn again, Daniel. Hurry up!

Daniel: Help me out, Han Jia! My foot is stuck!

Han Jia: Daniel became a snail ... time to lose some weight. This is truly "jin tui liang nan".

Fans: Hurry! "Jianchi bu xie."

Han Jia: Daniel, we have to make up for the lost time!

Daniel: Ok.Team Happy China must win!

Han Jia: I am really "dan qiang pi ma, fan shan yue ling, ba shan she shui"!

Fans: This is "qing er yi ju". Let's go! Hurry up!

Daniel: We've learned this at Hainan. He's actually saying it's easy.

场景 Scene 冒险岛

观　众：再接再厉，勇夺第一！快点，勇夺第一！

大　牛：这可真是步履维艰哪！

韩　佳：大牛，我们胜利在望！快，大牛！好，终于到了！

大　牛：可真是不容易！

韩　佳：下面马上就要轮到快乐观众队了，我们去看一看！

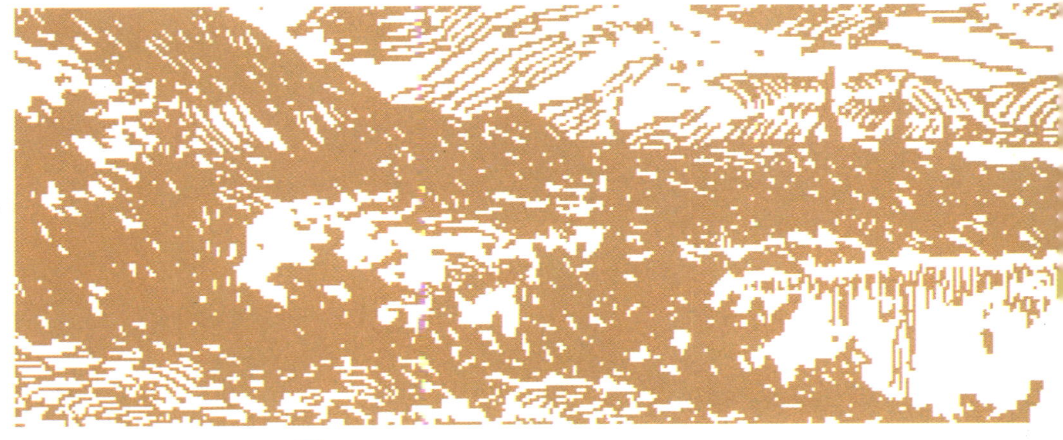

场景 Scene 冒险岛

裁　判：《快乐中国》队，你们一共用时是9分38秒，然而快乐观众队，你们完成所有的比赛项目，所使用的时间是9分28秒，但是在说成语和四字词语阶段，你们一共说了11个，而我们的快乐观众队一共说了6个。对，所以在说词阶段，是我们《快乐中国》队获胜！

大　牛：没错，《快乐中国》必胜！

裁　判：那么下面，我现在宣布：两队并列第一名！

韩　佳：今天的比赛可真是又紧张又刺激！

大　牛：真是开心极了！

韩　佳：我们《快乐中国》和观众朋友们永远是友谊第一，比赛第二！

Fans: "Zai jie zai li". Go for the first place! Hurry! Go for the first place!

Daniel: This is "bulü wei jian".

Han Jia: Daniel, "shengli zai wang"! Come on, Daniel! We're finally here.

Daniel: That was something.

Han Jia: Now it's Team Happy Fans' turn. Let's go and check it out.

The Judge: Team Happy China used 9 minutes 38 seconds. Team Happy Fans, in completing all the tasks, used 9 minutes 28 seconds! However, you guys came up with 11 idioms over all, while Team Happy Fans only had 6. So, Team Happy China wins the idiom portion of the match!

Daniel: Exactly. Team Happy China wins!

The Judge: So, I now declare ... both teams tie for the first place!

Han Jia: Today's match was intense and exciting!

Daniel: I'm so overjoyed!

Han Jia: Happy China and the fans believe in friendship first, competition second!

生词 New Words and Expressions

1.	成语	（名）	chéngyǔ	idiom
2.	信心	（名）	xìnxīn	confidence
3.	对……来说		duì……lái shuō	to . . . , it means . . .
4.	小试牛刀		xiǎo shì niú dāo	to display only one's small part of capability
5.	吹牛	（动）	chuīniú	to brag about
6.	轻松	（形）	qīngsōng	relaxed, light-hearted
7.	免得	（连）	miǎnde	in order not to, so as to avoid
8.	没劲儿	（形）	méijìnr	uninteresting
9.	耽误	（动）	dānwu	to miss, delay
10.	进退两难		jìn tuì liǎng nán	in a dilemma

注释 Notes

1. 对我大牛来说就是“小试牛刀”。

“对……来说……”这一结构表示从某人某事的角度来看。

The structure “对……来说……” means to look at something from the angle of a certain person or thing.

例如：对一个外国人来说，汉语说得这么好，真不容易。

2. 好了，大牛，该你了。

“该”，动词，在这里是“轮到”的意思。

“该”, a verb, here means “to take turns”.

例如：大牛，一会儿就该你表演节目了。

3. 刚才真是把我吓死了。

“死”在这里是形容词，用在某些动词或形容词后，表示达到极点。句尾多带助词"了"。

"死", an adjective here, is used after certain verbs or adjectives to indicate the extreme. Auxiliary word "了" is often put at the end of such sentences.

例如：这几天我忙死了，一点儿休息时间也没有。

4. "惊心动魄"就是形容非常紧张，把魂魄都给震动了。

"惊心动魄" means "soul-stirring" or "profoundly affected".

"都"，副词，在这里是"甚至"的意思。

"都", an adverb, here means "even".

例如：教室里一个人都没有，不知道他们上哪去了。

5. 你先歇会儿，免得待会儿没劲儿了。

"免得"，连词，表示避免发生某种不希望发生的情况，多用于后一个句子的开头。

"免得", a conjunction, is used to mean to avoid undesirable situations, and often begins the latter clause.

例如：你先给他打个电话，免得他着急。

6. 他还真摔倒了。

"还"，副词，在这里表示"没想到如此，而居然如此"。

"还", an adverb, is used here to indicate that something turns out to be like this unexpectedly.

例如：山这么高，他还真爬上去了。

7. 他竟然说这个容易！

"竟然"，副词，表示出乎意料。

"竟然", an adverb, expresses unexpectedness.

例如：没想到，大夫竟然把他的病治好了。

替换练习 Substitution Drills

1. 这个太简单了，对我来说就是	小试牛刀。		
	小菜一碟		
	举手之劳		
	手到病除		

2. 先	歇会儿，	免得	待会儿	没劲儿	了。
	吃一点儿		等会儿	饿	
	买一双		一会儿	卖完	
	打个电话		明天	忘	

3. 这可真是	进退两难	啊！
	哭笑不得	
	左右为难	
	大开眼界	

会话 Conversations

完成下列对话　Complete the following dialogues

（如括号里有词语或提示，请按要求做　Use the words or phrases given in the brackets）

A: 七点了，马力还没起来吧？

B: 可能还在睡觉呢！

A: 你去叫他一下儿，________________。（免得）

B: 今天再迟到，老师又得批评他了。

A: 今天的考试难吗？

B: ________________不太难。（对……来说）

A: 你是好学生，当然觉得不太难，别人觉得呢？

B: ________________。

世界之窗

【第一集】

场景 Scene 世界之窗

大　牛：韩佳，今天你又带我们到什么地方来了？

韩　佳：不就在你身后吗？深圳的世界之窗。

场景 Scene 伊什塔门（古巴比伦王国）

大　牛：韩佳，这里是什么地方？颜色这么艳丽呀！

韩　佳：这就是新巴比伦王国的伊什塔门。

大　牛：新巴比伦啊？

韩　佳：对呀！

大　牛：就是那个现在已经埋在沙漠里的王国啊？

韩　佳：没错，这新巴比伦王国啊……

大　牛：新巴比伦形成于“Tigris”和“Euphrates”之间的流域。[①]在那里，古老而智慧的人们，建造了当时世界上最美丽的城市。[②]那里的巴别塔和空中花园是当时辉煌的见证。

韩　佳：虽然它曾经辉煌，但是现在被埋在了沙漠底下。真是可惜呀！

Daniel: Han Jia. Where have you taken us today?

Han Jia: It's right behind you, Shenzhen's Window of the World.

Daniel: Where are we, Han Jia? The colors are so bright.

Han Jia: This is Ishtar Gate of New Babylon.

Daniel: New Babylon?

Han Jia: That's right.

Daniel: The kingdom that's already underneath the desert?

Han Jia: Exactly. This New Babylon ...

Daniel: New Babylon originated between Tigris and Euphrates Rivers. The ancient intelligent people built the world's most beautiful city at that time. Its Tower of Babel and Hanging Gardens were proof of their glory.

Han Jia: Although it used to be glorious, now it's all buried underneath the desert. What a pity.

场景 Scene 世界之窗内

大　牛：韩佳，刚才你用了“虽然……但是”说了一个复句。

韩　佳：大牛的耳朵还真尖，我刚才说了个复句他都听出来了。这对关联词“虽然……但是”是表示转折关系的。我们也可以说：“虽然大牛不是中国人，但是他会说中文。”

Suīrán Dà Niú bú shì Zhōngguórén，dànshì tā huì shuō Zhōngwén.
虽然 大 牛 不 是 中国人， 但是 他 会 说 中 文。

Although he's not Chinese, Daniel speaks Chinese.

大　牛：韩佳，刚才你说我的耳朵尖的。我的耳朵哪里长得尖？③ 你说！

韩　佳：我说的尖呀，不是“细小、尖锐”的意思，而是指“灵敏”。我刚才是在夸你耳朵灵敏，听得认真仔细。

大　牛：早说嘛！

Daniel: Han Jia, you used "although ..." to form a compound sentence.

Han Jia: Daniel's ears are really "jian". He noticed the compound sentence I used. The words "suiran ... danshi" expresses a transitional relationship. We could also say, although Daniel's not Chinese, he could speak Chinese.

Daniel: Han Jia, you said my ears were "jian". How are they pointy?

Han Jia: I didn't mean thin and pointy by that. It means keen and sensitive. I meant to praise you for having keen ears and a good understanding.

Daniel: Now I get it.

场景 Scene 世界之窗内

韩　佳：大牛，这里呀，一共有六扇门④。分别是巴比伦门、埃及门、印度门、中华门、太阳门和伊斯兰门。你知道它们代表什么吗？

大　牛：这你可难不倒我。它们分别代表的是古巴比伦、古埃及、古印度、古中国四大文明古国，以及古老的印第安、伊斯兰文化。

韩　佳：没错！

Han Jia: Daniel, there are a total of six gates here. They are the Gate of Babylon, Gate of Egypt, Gate of India, Gate of China, Gate of Sun and Gate of Islam. Do you know what they symbolize?

Daniel: You can't get me with this. They represent four ancient kingdoms of Babylon, Egypt, India, China respectively, and the ancient Indian and Islamic cultures.

Han Jia: Very good.

场景 Scene 世界之窗 巴黎

大　牛：哎呀，我简直是不敢相信！韩佳，这不是来到了法国巴黎吗？

韩　佳：大牛，这是深圳世界之窗的景观之一，巴黎四大洲喷泉。

大　牛：实在是太像了！还有我们身后的凯旋门、埃菲尔铁塔，我以为真来到了巴黎呢⑤！韩佳，有一个形容词，是形容特别特别像真的，怎么说来着⑥？

韩　佳：逼真？

大　牛：没错，“逼真”，都读一声，形容非常像真的。

韩　佳：“逼真”就是形容非常像真的。比如：“雕塑中的人物多么地逼真。”

Diāosù zhōng de rénwù duōme bīzhēn.

雕塑 中 的人物 多么 逼真。

The figures in the sculpture are very lifelike.

Daniel: Wow, I can't believe it. We've arrived in Paris of France.

Han Jia: Daniel, this is one of the spots in the Window of World. Paris' Fountain of the Four Continents.

Daniel: It looks so real. And the Triumphal Arch and Eiffel Tower behind us. I thought we're really in Paris. Han Jia, there's an adjective that means extremely real ...

Han Jia: "Bizhen?"

Daniel: Yes, that's right. "Bizhen", two first tones, means strikingly realistic.

Han Jia: "Bi zhen" describes something very real. For example, the sculpted figures are very realistic.

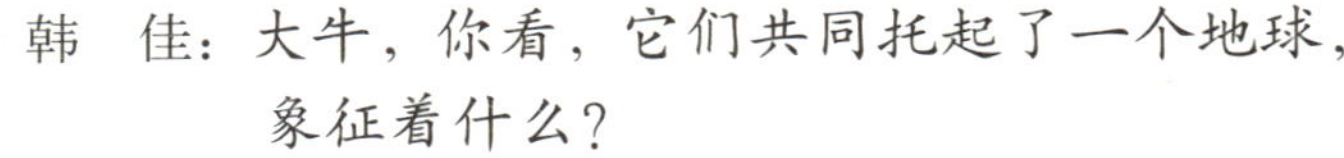

韩　佳：大牛，你看，它们共同托起了一个地球，象征着什么？

大　牛：我想应该是象征着四大洲的人们团结和平，友好相处吧？

韩　佳：没错，就是欧、亚、美、非四大洲。

大　牛：你看，这上面是马，这下面是什么呢？

韩　佳：鱼尾。

大　牛：是海豚的尾巴。马和海豚象征着陆地与海洋的结合，也代表着力量与智慧的结合。

韩　佳：大牛，有长进，不但会解释，还说出个复句来。

大　牛：又是一个复句呀？

韩　佳：嗯！用“也”连接的复句表示并列关系。我们还可以说：“我今天很开心，大牛也是。”

Han Jia: Look, Daniel. They are holding up a globe. What does it symbolize?

Daniel: I think it symbolizes peace and harmony among people of the four continents.

Han Jia: Yes. Europe, Asia, Americas, and Africa.

Daniel: Look, the top is a horse, what's the bottom?

Han Jia: Fish tail?

Daniel: Nope, it's a dolphin tail. Horses and dolphins symbolize the harmony between land and sea, as well as the combination of power and wisdom.

Han Jia: Not bad, Daniel. You used a compound sentence in your explanation.

Daniel: Another compound sentence?

Han Jia: Yes. A compound sentence connected by "ye" expresses a relationship of juxtaposition. We can also say, "I'm very happy today, so is Daniel".

场景 Scene 晚会表演

大　牛：我觉得这里的夜晚更美。你们瞧，我们身后的这座大圣诞树，多漂亮！不过，我看着怎么这么眼熟啊？

韩　佳：这么快你就忘了，这不就是我们白天看到的埃菲尔铁塔吗？

大　牛：白天看塔，晚上看树，设计得真巧妙！

韩　佳：大牛，你听，好像是世界之窗的晚会表演开始了，我们去看看！

Shìjiè Zhī Chuāng de wǎnhuì biǎoyǎn kāishǐ le.

世界之窗的晚会表演开始了。

The evening performance at Window of the World has started.

场景 Scene 晚会表演

大　牛：这里的表演真是太精彩了！

韩　佳：这些演员可真不简单哪！

大　牛：真想上去和她们一起演哪！

韩　佳：大牛，你可别捣乱啊！

大　牛：什么呀，来吧！

Daniel: I think the night is even more beautiful here. Look at the giant Christmas tree behind us. Isn't it pretty? How come it looks so familiar?

Han Jia: Have you already forgotten? It's what we saw earlier today, the Eiffel Tower.

Daniel: Tower in the day, tree at night. Very well designed.

Han Jia: Listen, Daniel... Sounds like the evening performance here has started. Let's go.

Daniel: The performances are amazing!

Han Jia: These actors are truly great!

Daniel: Wish I could go up the stage with them.

Han Jia: Don't mess around, Daniel.

Daniel: Let's just do it!

场景 Scene 舞台上

韩　佳：大牛！

大　牛：韩佳，虽然我不能上台和演员一起表演，但是我可以站在这里，向观众朋友们告别，让他们永远记住来到世界之窗的这一天。

韩　佳：没错，世界之窗的口号是：

合：您给我一天，我给您一个世界！

Han Jia: Daniel ...

Daniel: Han Jia, although I can't perform with the actors, I can stand here and say goodbye to our friends. Let them remember this day at Window of the World forever.

Han Jia: Yes. Its slogan is:

Together : You give me a day, and I'll give you a world.

生词 New Words and Expressions

1. 智慧	（名）	zhìhuì	wisdom
2. 形成	（动）	xíngchéng	to form
3. 辉煌	（形）	huīhuáng	glorious, brilliant
4. 雕塑	（名）	diāosù	sculpture
5. 逼真	（形）	bīzhēn	true to life, vivid
6. 地球	（名）	dìqiú	the earth
7. 眼熟	（形）	yǎnshú	familiar
8. 设计	（动、名）	shèjì	to design; design
9. 巧妙	（形）	qiǎomiào	clever, ingenious
10. 精彩	（形）	jīngcǎi	excellent, marvelous

注释 Notes

1. 新巴比伦形成于“Tigris”和“Euphrates”之间的流域。

“于”，介词，用在动词后可表示处所或时间，是“在”的意思，用于书面语。

“于”, a preposition, is used after a verb denoting the place or time, meaning “in; at; on; from”, and used in written Chinese.

例如：我1990年毕业于北京大学。（处所）
　　　他出生于1985年。（时间）

2. 在那里，古老而智慧的人们，建造了当时世界上最美丽的城市。

“而”，连词，在这里连接两个并列的形容词，表示互相补充。

“而”, a conjunction, is used to link two coordinate adjectives, complementing each other.

例如：这篇文章短小而生动，很值得看。

3. 我的耳朵哪里长得尖？

这是一个反问句，用肯定的形式表示否定的意思。“哪里”在这里不表示处所，只表示反问语气。

This is a rhetorical question, affirmative in form but negative in meaning. “哪里” does not refer to place but indicates the rhetorical tone.

例如：他哪里是美国人，他是加拿大人。

4．这里呀，一共有六**扇**门。

“扇”，在这里用做“门”或“窗”的量词。

“扇” is often used as a measure word for “door” or “window”.

例如：你数一数这个房子有几扇门、几扇窗户。

5．我**以为**真来到了巴黎呢！

“以为”，动词，对人或事物作出某种论断，但所作出的论断常常不符合事实，需要用另一个句子指明真相。

“以为”，a verb, is used to indicate one' s judgment, which, however, is often contrary to the fact. Another sentence is required to point out the truth.

例如：我们都以为你已经走了，原来你还没走啊！

6．怎么说**来着**？

“来着”，助词，用在句尾，表示曾经发生过什么事情，用于口语。

“来着”， an auxiliary word, used at the end of a sentence and in spoken Chinese, indicates what has happened.

例如：昨天张小姐跟你说什么来着？

替换练习 Substitution Drills

1．虽然	大牛	不是	中国人，但是	他会说中文。
	我		他朋友	我了解他
	他		年轻人	他理解年轻人
	姐姐		画家	她能画上几笔

2. 雕塑中	的	人物	多么	逼真。
马路上		汽车		拥挤
森林里		树木		茂密
幼儿园里		孩子		可爱

3. 世界之窗	的	晚会	表演开始了。
欢迎新生		节目	
艺术团		文艺	
杂技团		精彩	

会话 Conversations

完成下列对话　Complete the following dialogues
(如括号里有词语或提示，请按要求做　Use the words or phrases given in the brackets)

A: 你去过美国吧?
B: 我 ______________。(用"哪里"反问)
A: 那你去年去的是……
B: 我去年去的是加拿大，我还没去过美国呢!

A: 他是你哥哥吧?
B: 不，他是我弟弟。
A: 你们两个人长得差不多，我 ______________。(以为)
B: 我比他大两岁。

世界之窗

【第二集】

场景 Scene 世界之窗内　亚洲建筑

韩　佳：大牛，你干吗呢？

大　牛：我在想，这里怎么有这么多东方的建筑呢①？

韩　佳：今天我就要带你去看看亚洲的名胜古迹。

场景 Scene 泰姬陵

大　牛：韩佳，这是什么地方？美得像一座宫殿。

韩　佳：这不是宫殿，而是陵墓。

Zhè bú shì gōngdiàn, ér shì língmù.

这 不 是 宫殿，而 是 陵墓。

This isn't a palace, it's a tomb.

Han Jia: What are you doing, Daniel?

Daniel: I'm wondering why there are so many Oriental architecture here.

Han Jia: Today, I'm taking you to see famous Asian attractions.

Daniel: What is this, Han Jia? A beautiful palace?

Han Jia: No, this is not a palace, it's a tomb.

场景 Scene 泰姬陵

大　牛：韩佳，怎么会有这么漂亮的陵墓呢？

韩　佳：这泰姬陵是印度的一颗珍珠，背后还有一个凄美的爱情故事。

大　牛：还有故事，韩佳，快说给我听听！

韩　佳：想听故事，那就先回答我一个问题。

大　牛：还有条件？快问吧！

韩　佳：有一位军事统帅叫成吉思汗。

大　牛：哎呀，太简单了！他叫成吉思汗，他是蒙古帝国的开国君主。

韩　佳：这大牛，历史倒是学得不错，不过名字中最重要的一个字，他念错了。②应该是成吉思汗。这"汗"和"汗"虽然写法相同，但是读第二声"汗"的时候，是表示对一种职位的尊称。

大　牛：哦！我知道了，成吉思汗。成吉思汗和泰姬有什么关系？

韩　佳：这泰姬所在的莫卧儿王朝，就是成吉思汗的后代建立的。③

大　牛：哦，原来如此！

Daniel: How could a tomb be so beautiful?

Han Jia: The Taj Mahal is a pearl of India. There's also a touching love story behind it.

Daniel: A story? Come on, tell me...

Han Jia: Well, you'll have to answer a question first.

Daniel: A question? Okay, shoot...

Han Jia: There was a military leader named Genghis Khan ...

Daniel: This is easy ... His name was Genghis Khan. He was the first emperor of the Mongol Empire of the Middle Ages .

Han Jia: Daniel really knows his history, but he mispronounced a key word. It should be "Chengjisihan", second tone. Although the two "han" characters look the same, when it's pronounced the second tone, it refers to a kind of honorable rank.

Daniel: Now I get it, "Chengjisihan". But what's Genghis Khan got to do with Taj Mahal?

Han Jia: The Mughal Dynasty was built by Genghis Khan's offsprings.

Daniel: Oh, I see...

场景 Scene 泰姬陵

大　牛：故事现在可以开始讲了吧？

韩　佳：瞧把你急的！这莫卧儿王朝第五代帝王沙杰汗有一个美丽而又忠诚的妻子，叫泰姬玛哈尔。他们俩相依相伴一起生活了几十年，但不幸的是泰姬难产死了。她临终前向她的爱人提出了一个要求：那就是为她建造一座最美丽的陵墓。于是，悲伤的沙杰汗，就在他的爱妻死后建造了这样一座美丽的陵墓。④你看，这上面镂空的雕花，还有这些石柱，可以想象，当时建造的时候是多么地细致、用心啊！

大　牛：怪不得这是伊斯兰建筑中的一大奇迹呢！

Zhè shì Yīsīlán jiànzhù zhōng de yí gè qíjì.

这 是 伊斯兰 建筑 中 的 一 个 奇迹。

This is a miracle in Islamic architecture.

Daniel: Can you start the story now?

Han Jia: Look how impatient you are. The Mughal Dynasty's fifth emperor, Shah Jahan, had a beautiful and loyal wife named Taj Mahal. The two of them lived together for many decades. But unfortunately, his wife died at childbirth. She made a dying wish to her husband to build here the most beautiful tomb. So, the sad Shah Jahan built this magnificent tomb for his wife after she died. Look at these through-carved flowers and the stone columns. You can just imagine how meticulously designed it was.

Daniel: No wonder this is a miracle of Islamic architecture.

场景 Scene　微缩婆罗浮屠

大　牛：我说，韩佳，这就是你说的更好看的？

韩　佳：对呀！

大　牛：这么小，是什么呀？

韩　佳：实际的可不小。它是按1比15的比例缩小的，这是印度尼西亚的婆罗浮屠。这可是世界上最大的佛教建筑之一。

大　牛：是吗？那我可得好好看看。这里面密密麻麻的都是小石雕，而且每个人的表情、动作都不一样。

韩　佳：这上面都是一个个佛教故事⑤，还有世俗人民的生活，一共有两千七百多幅呢！

大　牛：这么多！这婆罗浮屠里面的"浮屠"是什么意思啊？

韩　佳：古代人把佛塔叫做浮屠。那信仰佛教的人希望把佛塔修建得越高越好。

大　牛：我说怎么听着这么耳熟呢！这回我想起来了，是不是有一句话叫做"救人一命，胜造七级浮屠"？

韩　佳：没错，意思就是说救人一命胜过造了七层高的佛塔。

大　牛：*意思就是说救人一命胜过造了七层高的佛塔。*

韩　佳：大牛，你看！那边有一片樱花特别好看，我们去看看！

Daniel: Hey, Han Jia. Is this what you were talking about?

Han Jia: Yep.

Daniel: It's so small...

Han Jia: The actual thing is not small. This model is built on a 1:15 ratio. This is Indonesia's Borobudur. It's one of the world's largest Buddhist architecture.

Daniel: Really? I've got to check it out. The inside is filled with countless stone sculptures. Each figure has a different expression and pose.

Han Jia: And each one tells a Buddhist story or a folk tale of everyday life. There are more than 2,700 of them.

Daniel: Amazing ... What exactly does the term "futu" mean?

Han Jia: The ancients called a Buddhist pagoda "futu." Buddhist believers think that the taller the "futu" the better it is.

Daniel: No wonder it sounded so familiar. Now I remember. Isn't there a saying that says, "jiu ren yi ming, sheng zao qi ji futu".

Han Jia: That's right. It means that saving a life is better than building a seven-story pagoda.

Daniel: It means that saving someone's life is even better than building a seven-story Buddhist tower.

Han Jia: Look, Daniel. There are some pretty cherry blossoms. Let's go check it out.

场景 Scene 日本皇家园林

韩　佳：没想到这么快我就站在日本的皇家园林中了！

大　牛：这里既自然古朴又清新雅致。

Zhèli jì zìrán gǔpǔ yòu qīngxīn yǎzhì.

这里 既 自然 古朴 又 清新 雅致。

This place is natural and elegant.

韩　佳：你看，你用"既……又……"说了一个复句，用这对关联词的复句是表示并列关系的。

大　牛：对，比如说："我大牛既聪明又帅气。"

韩　佳：这句子倒是说得没错，但是你总也改不掉既爱自作聪明，又爱吹牛的毛病⑥。

Han Jia: I can't believe we're already in a Japanese imperial garden.

Daniel: It's very natural yet very elegant.

Han Jia: You just used a "ji ... you ..." compound sentence. Such compound sentences express a relationship of juxtaposition.

Daniel: For example, Daniel is smart as well as handsome.

Han Jia: The grammar is correct, but you still haven't stopped your tendency to brag all the time.

世界之窗

场景 Scene 东南亚水乡

大　牛：韩佳，这里就特别像中国云南兄弟民族居住的地方。

韩　佳：这里是东南亚水乡。泰国、缅甸、马来西亚等国家都属于这个范围。这里的建筑和我们中国云南有相似之处。

大　牛：你看，那些女孩子，她们穿的裙子就和中国傣族姑娘穿的竹筒裙很像。

韩　佳：你呀，别研究了！

Daniel: Han Jia, this looks just like the residence of Yunnan's ethnic groups.

Han Jia: This is Southeast Asia's water region. Thailand, Burma and Malaysia all belong to this region. The styles of architecture here are similar to those of Yunnan.

Daniel: Look at those girls ... their dresses look like the bamboo-tube dresses of Chinese Dai girls.

Han Jia: Stop scrutinizing the girls.

生词 New Words and Expressions

1.	名胜古迹		míngshèng gǔjì	scenic spots and historic relics
2.	宫殿	（名）	gōngdiàn	palace
3.	陵墓	（名）	língmù	mausoleum
4.	忠诚	（形）	zhōngchéng	loyal
5.	悲伤	（形）	bēishāng	sad, sorrowful
6.	细致	（形）	xìzhì	meticulous
7.	奇迹	（名）	qíjì	miracle
8.	古朴	（形）	gǔpǔ	simple and unsophisticated
9.	雅致	（形）	yǎzhì	refined, tasteful
10.	属于	（动）	shǔyú	to belong to

注释 Notes

1. 这里怎么有这么多东方的建筑呢？

"怎么"在这里用于询问原因，等于"为什么"。

"怎么" is used here to ask for the reason, equivalent to "why".

例如：他今天怎么这样高兴？

2. 这大牛，历史倒是学得不错，不过名字中最重要的一个字，他念错了。

"倒是"，副词，在这里表示让步，后面的句子常用"但是""就是""不过"等呼应。

"倒是", an adverb, here is used to imply concession, and what follows are often such expressions like "但是""就是""不过" to echo with it.

例如：这儿的环境倒是不错，就是交通不太方便。

3. 这泰姬所在的莫卧儿王朝，就是成吉思汗的后代建立的。

当一个动作发生在过去，而我们现在要着重指出那个动作发生的时间、地点、方式等，就可以用"是……的"这种结构。

The structure "是……的" is used to point out emphatically the time, place or manner of an action took place in the past.

例如：他们是昨天来的。（时间）

我是从北京来的。（地点）

他是骑自行车来的。（方式）

这些菜是妈妈做的。（施事者）

否定式是："不是……的"。

例如：飞机票不是我买的。

4. 于是，悲伤的沙杰汗，就在他的爱妻死后建造了这样一座美丽的陵墓。

"于是"，连词，表示后一事件承接前一事件，后一事件往往是由前一事件引起的。

"于是", a conjunction, is used to show what happens later directly following the former in cident and is also caused by the former.

例如：大家一致鼓励他参加全校的游泳比赛，于是他决定去报名。

5. 这上面都是一个个佛教故事。

现代汉语里，数词"一"加量词可以重叠，重叠后第二个"一"可以省略。这种重叠的数量词组的作用在于描写。

In modern Chinese, the numeral "一" plus a measure word can be repeated, and in the repeated form, the second "一" can be omitted.

例如：看着面前这一张张熟悉的面孔，他感到亲切极了。

6. 但是你总也改不掉既爱自作聪明，又爱吹牛的毛病。

"总"，副词，表示"一直""一向"的意思。

"总", an adverb, means "always", "consistently".

例如：每天吃完晚饭以后他总要去散步。

替换练习 Substitution Drills

1. 这	不是	宫殿，	而是	陵墓。
他		中国人		韩国人
我		他舅舅		他叔叔
这里		教学楼		宿舍楼

2. 这是	伊斯兰建筑	中的一	个	奇迹。
	物理学		组	术语
	沙漠		种	现象
	绝望		线	希望

3.	这里	既	自然古朴	又	清新雅致。
	他		严肃		有礼貌
	那里		开阔		安静
	北京		古老		年轻

会话 Conversations

完成下列对话　Complete the following dialogues
（如括号里有词语或提示，请按要求做　Use the words or phrases given in the brackets）

A: 陈东在吗？
B: 不在，他去锻炼了。
A: 他每天下午都要锻炼吗？
B: 没错，______。（总）

A: 今天的展览会怎么样？
B: ______。（倒是……就是……）
A: 今天是星期天，人肯定多。
B: 所以你们不要星期六星期天去，人实在是太多了。

世界之窗

【第三集】

场景 Scene　世界之窗　英国景区

韩　佳：大家好！这里是《快乐中国》，我是快乐的韩佳！怎么就我一个人在这里说话？[①]大牛呢？

大　牛：快乐的大牛在这儿呢！韩佳，我来了！

韩　佳：你在那迷宫一样的地方转来转去干吗呢？[②]

大　牛：哦！那是"the Mazes"，英国非常有特色的一种娱乐设施。

韩　佳：是到了大牛的家乡了，怪不得你那么兴奋呢！

大　牛：韩佳，你手中的这玫瑰花是准备送给谁的？

韩　佳：这是别人送给我的。《罗马假日》中的公主就是这样，手持鲜花站在这里。你不会没看过《罗马假日》吧？[③]

大　牛：这么经典的一部影片，我怎么没看过？咱们身后的不就是电影中的场景吗？

韩　佳：可是为什么意大利的建筑要叫西班牙大台阶呢？

大　牛：这是因为17世纪的时候，这儿附近有西班牙大使馆，所以才得此名。

韩　佳："因为……所以……"，大牛，考考你，这是什么关系的复句？

大　牛：这你可考不倒我，"因为……所以……"表示因果关系。"因为"表示原因，"所以"表示结果。因为见到了英国的建筑，所以我特别高兴。

Yīnwèi　jiàndàole　Yīngguó　de　jiànzhù，suǒyǐ　wǒ　tèbié　gāoxìng．

因为　见到了　英国　的　建筑，所以　我　特别　高兴。

I'm very excited because I saw some British architecture.

Han Jia: Hello, everyone. Welcome to *Happy China*. I am happy Han Jia. Why am I the only one who is talking? Where is Daniel?

Daniel: Happy Daniel is here. Han Jia, I'm here.

Han Jia: Why are you wandering around a place like a maze?

Daniel: Oh, that's the Mazes. It is a very typical amusement facility in Britain.

Han Jia: We have come to Daniel's hometown. No wonder you are so excited.

Daniel: Hey, Han Jia, to whom are you going to present the roses in your hands?

Han Jia: It's a present from somebody. The princess in *Roman Holiday* is holding a bouquet and standing here like this. Have you ever seen *Roman Holiday*?

Daniel: How can I miss such a classic movie? Isn't the scene behind us in the movie?

Han Jia: But why is Italian architecture called Spanish Step?

Daniel: It is because in the 17th century, there was a Spanish embassy around here. Hence it got its name.

Han Jia: " Yonwei...suoyi...". Daniel, I have a question for you. What kind of complex sentence is it?

Daniel: It is easy. " Yonwei...suoyi..." indicates causality. " Yinwei" means cause and " Suoyi" means effect. I saw British architecture, so I was very pleased.

世界之窗

大　牛：那里还有很多英国建筑，咱们过去看看吧！

韩　佳：瞧把你急的，是不是归心似箭了？

大　牛：没错，“归心似箭”就是形容想回家的心情像射出去的箭一样急速。“归心似箭。”

韩　佳：“归心似箭”就是形容想回家的心情像射出去的箭一样急速。大牛，去你家看看！

大　牛：走！

场景 Scene　英国微缩建筑

大　牛：啊！到家了。站在这里感觉真亲切，好像回到了家一样，就是觉得自己好像变大了好几倍呀④！

韩　佳：那当然了！微缩的嘛，站在这里当然有一种巨人的感觉了。

大　牛：看，白金汉宫、伦敦塔桥，还有大笨钟。

Daniel: There are so many British structures over there. Let's go over and take a look.

Han Jia: You are in such a hurry. Can't you wait to go back home?

Daniel: Right. " Gui xin si jian" means to feel a sudden longing to return home. " Gui xin si jian".

Han Jia: " Gui xin si jian" means the eagerness of going back home, which is as swift as a shooting arrow. Daniel, let's go to your home to take a look.

Daniel: Come on.

Daniel: Wow, home again. It is so intimate to stand here. I feel like going back home. I feel like several times bigger.

Han Jia: Of course. They are miniatures. You will certainly feel like a giant when you stand here.

Daniel: Look, here are mini Buckingham Palace and London Bridge. Look, over there, it's Big Ben!

场景 Scene 大笨钟

大　牛：这就是。

韩　佳：什么？Big Ben不就是大笨钟吗？是你们英国国会大厦的主要标志。

大　牛：韩佳懂得真多。实际的大笨钟要比这个大上十几倍呢！

韩　佳：大牛，那边那片花园是你们英国的吗？好像不太像，咱们过去看看。

韩　佳：好啊！

场景 Scene 凡尔赛宫

大　牛：这就是美丽的凡尔赛。

韩　佳：哦，这就是法国的凡尔赛宫啊！据说是路易十四为自己建造的一座豪华皇宫。

大　牛：说得没错，这就是欧洲最宏伟、最华丽的宫殿。它既有古典主义的布局，又有巴洛克式的装饰风格。

韩　佳：大牛，说得头头是道啊！

Dà Niú shuō de tóu tóu shì dào.

大 牛 说 得 头 头 是 道。

Daniel has put it to a "T".

Daniel: This is it.

Han Jia: Is it Big Ben? It's the symbol of House of Parliament.

Daniel: Hey, Han Jia really knows a lot. The real one is more than ten times bigger than this.

Han Jia: Daniel, is the garden over there British? Well, it does not look like British. Let's go and check it out.

Han Jia: All right.

Daniel: It is the beautiful Versailles.

Han Jia: Oh, so it is France's Versailles. It is said to be a magnificent palace built by Louis XIV for himself.

Daniel: Exactly. It is the most splendid and most magnificent palace in Europe. It has both the classic layout and the Baroque style.

Han Jia: Wow, Daniel knows a lot.

场景 Scene 新天鹅堡

韩　佳：站在这里就感觉自己像童话中的白雪公主一样。

大　牛：还自我陶醉呢！这里就是位于德国南部的Neuschwanstein，新天鹅堡。迪斯尼的标志是以它为原形创作的。⑤

韩　佳：这座城堡据说是建筑师根据一位音乐家创作的音乐意境而设计的⑥，神奇不神奇？

大　牛：音乐意境！有句话是这么说的："*音乐是流动的建筑，建筑是凝固的音乐。*"

韩　佳：音乐是流动的建筑，建筑是凝固的音乐。

Jiànzhù　shì　nínggù　de yīnyuè.

建筑　是　凝固　的 音乐。

Architecture is frozen music.

Han Jia: I feel like Snow White in the fairy tale when I stand here.

Daniel: You are enchanted. This is the Neuschwanstein Castle located in southern Germany. The symbol of Disney was designed using it as a model.

Han Jia: The castle is said to be designed according to the music sense of a composer. Is it marvelous?

Daniel: Hey, music sense. A saying goes like this: Music is like flowing architecture and architecture is like frozen music.

Han Jia: Music is like flowing architecture and architecture is like frozen music.

场景 Scene 圣马可广场

韩　佳：大牛，你干吗呢？这是什么地方啊？

大　牛：这里就是威尼斯的圣马可广场，我在脱帽行礼呢！

韩　佳：这么虔诚啊！可是，你为什么要在广场上行礼呢？

大　牛：这个广场可不一般，这里是最能代表威尼斯繁华和悠久历史的地方。拿破仑第一次来到这儿的时候，就脱帽、鞠躬、行礼，表示尊敬。

韩　佳：就像你刚才那样？

大　牛：大概是吧！他说这里是全欧洲最高雅的客厅。

韩　佳：这个评价可够高的。

场景 Scene 圣马可广场

韩　佳：大牛，你觉没觉得这里的装饰有些东方的特色？

大　牛：对，威尼斯的地理位置很特殊，所以这里融合了东西方文化。

韩　佳：你看，咱俩走在这圣马可广场里，不就是一幅典型的东西方文化融合的画面吗？

大　牛：嗯！这个画面多美呀，真是舍不得离开这里。

Han Jia: Daniel, what are you doing? Where is it?

Daniel: It is the St. Marco Plaza in Venice. I am saluting.

Han Jia: You are so pious. But why did you salute on the plaza?

Daniel: Hey, it is not an ordinary plaza. It is the place that best represents the prosperity and long history of Venice. When Napoleon first came here, he took off his hat, bowed and saluted to show his respect.

Han Jia: Just like what you did.

Daniel: Maybe. He said it was the most elegant living room in the entire Europe.

Han Jia: He really thought highly of it.

Han Jia: Daniel, do you think the decoration here is somewhat Oriental?

Daniel: Yes. The geographical location of Venice is very special. So it combines the Eastern and Western cultures.

Han Jia: Look, the two of us walking on St. Marco Plaza is a typical picture combining Eastern and Western cultures.

Daniel: Well, the scene is so beautiful. I am really reluctant to leave.

生词 New Words and Expressions

1．娱乐	（名）	yú lè	entertainment
2．形容	（动）	xíngróng	to describe
3．亲切	（形）	qīnqiè	kind, close
4．风格	（名）	fēnggé	style
5．头头是道		tóu tóu shì dào	clear and logical, utterly convincing
6．根据	（动、名）	gēnjù	to depend on; grounds
7．凝固	（动）	nínggù	to solidify
8．悠久	（形）	yōujiǔ	long-standing
9．融合	（动）	rónghé	to merge, fuse

注释 Notes

1．怎么就我一个人在这里说话？

"就"，副词，在这里表示确定范围，相当于"只"。

"就"，an adverb, defines the range, meaning "only".

例如：昨天爬山就他一个人没去。

2．你在那迷宫一样的地方转来转去干吗呢？

"动词＋来＋动词＋去"这一结构表示动作的多次重复。

The structure "verb+ 来 +verb+ 去" means repeated actions.

例如：昨天开会，大家讨论来讨论去，终于把计划定下来了。

"干吗"，意思是"干什么"，用于询问原因或目的。

"干吗"，meaning "whatever for", is used to ask for reasons or purposes.

例如：大家都知道了，你说这些干吗呢？

3．你不会没看过《罗马假日》吧？

"不……没（有）……"这是一种双重否定的结构，表示肯定的意思。

"不……没（有）……" is a double negative structure, having an affirmative meaning.

例如：明天上午参观服装展览会，李小姐不会没通知你吧？

4. **就是觉得自己好像变大了好几倍呀!**

"好"，副词，这里用在数词前，强调多。

"好", an adverb, is used here before the numeral "几" to emphasize large quantities.

例如：今年我们公司新来了好几个人。

5. **迪斯尼的标志是以它为原形创作的。**

"以……为……"这一结构相当于"把……作为……"。

The structure "以……为……" is equivalent to the structure "把……作为……".

例如：明天参观的地方以山上的景点为主，如果有时间再看别的。

6. **这座城堡据说是建筑师根据一位音乐家创作的音乐意境而设计的。**

"而"，连词，它在句子中的作用是连接表示依据的成分和动词。

"而", a conjunction, links the previously mentioned element with the verb after it.

例如：这个计划是根据大家的意见而制订出来的。

替换练习 Substitution Drills

1. 因为 见到 了 英国 的 建筑，所以 我特别高兴。
   接到 爸爸 来信 他十分高兴
   受到 寒流 影响 这里很冷
   看到 对方 邀请函 大家都很兴奋

2. 大牛 说 得 头头是道。
   他 讲 娓娓动听
   他们 唱 悦耳动听
   大伙 吃 酒足饭饱

3. 建筑 是 凝固 的 音乐。
   人民 国家 主人
   孩子 妈妈 希望
   伦敦 英国 首都

会话 Conversations

完成下列对话 Complete the following dialogues

(如括号里有词语或提示,请按要求做 Use the words or phrases given in the brackets)

A: 那个电影你觉得怎么样?

B: 很不错，你这个电影迷，早看过了吧?

A: 我很喜欢那个电影，已经 ________________。(好)

B: 有机会我也想再看一遍。

A: 他们提出的问题解决了吗?

B: 没有呢!

A: 再想想吧!

B: 我想了一天了，但是 ________________。(……来……去)

世界之窗

【第四集】

场景 Scene　尼亚加拉大瀑布

韩　佳：大牛，今天咱们是不是该去美洲了①？

大　牛：怎么被你猜到了。

韩　佳：那还用猜呀，咱们身后不就是尼亚加拉大瀑布吗？

大　牛：说得没错，这里就是位于美国和加拿大交界处的尼亚加拉大瀑布。

韩　佳：没错，这可是世界七大奇景之一，虽然被缩小了很多倍，但是看上去仍然很壮观②。

大　牛：今天我们就从这里走进美洲去看看，走！

Han Jia: Hey, Daniel, are we going to America today?

Daniel: Hey, you got it.

Han Jia: It is easy. Isn't it the Niagara Falls behind us?

Daniel: You are right. This is the Niagara Falls on the border of the United States and Canada.

Han Jia: Right. It is one of the world's seven great views. Although it is many times smaller, it still looks magnificent.

Daniel: Today we will start from here and go to America to take a look. Let's go.

场景 Scene　华盛顿

大　牛：现在我们来到了美国的华盛顿。

韩　佳：这是美国的政治中心，怪不得这里的建筑都那么庄严肃穆呢！

大　牛：嗯！这里有白宫，有国会大厦，还有 Mount Rushmore National Memorial。

韩　佳：就是总统山吧？

大　牛：没错！

Zhèli yǒu Báigōng, yǒu Guóhuì Dàshà, hái yǒu Zǒngtǒngshān.
这里 有 白宫，有 国会 大厦，还 有 总统山。

There's the White House, Capitol and Mount Rushmore.

大　牛：韩佳，你认得他们吗？

韩　佳：哦！华盛顿、杰斐逊、西奥多罗斯福和林肯。这四位可是美国历史上非常重要的人物。不过，把他们的头像刻在山上，让后人世代敬仰，这也算得上是独出心裁了吧③？

大　牛："独出心裁"，是不是独自想出一个新颖的材料的意思啊？

韩　佳："心裁"，是指内心的设计和筹划。"独出心裁"就是指独自一个人想出一个与众不同的办法来。

大　牛：*"独出心裁"就是指独自一个人想出一个与众不同的办法来。*"独出心裁。"

韩　佳：大牛，那是自由女神像吧？我们过去看看！

大　牛：走！

Daniel: Hey, now we are in Washington D. C. in the U.S.

Han Jia: It is the political center of the U.S. No wonder the buildings here are so solemn and grand.

Daniel: Right. There are White House and Capitol, and Mount Rushmore National Memorial.

Han Jia: Is it Mount Rushmore?

Daniel: Right.

Daniel: Hey, Han Jia, do you know them?

Han Jia: Oh, Washington, Jefferson, Theodore Roosevelt and Lincoln. They are very important figures in American history. But it is also creative to carve their head portraits on the hill for the offsprings to worship, isn't it?

Daniel: Does "du chu xincai" mean thinking of a creative material by oneself?

Han Jia: "Xincai" means inner design and planning. "Du chu xincai" means thinking of a novel method by oneself.

Daniel: "Du chu xincai" means to think of a new and unique method."Du chu xincai".

Han Jia: Daniel, is that Statue of Liberty? Let's go over and check it out.

Daniel: Let's go.

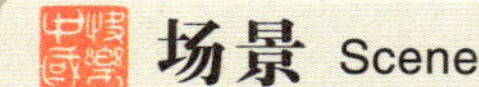

场景 Scene 微缩自由女神

大　牛：这自由女神像是美国的标志之一，美国独立100周年的时候法国送给美国的一份礼物。

韩　佳：大牛，你看那边！那不是复活节岛吗？怎么那么快就到了南美洲了？

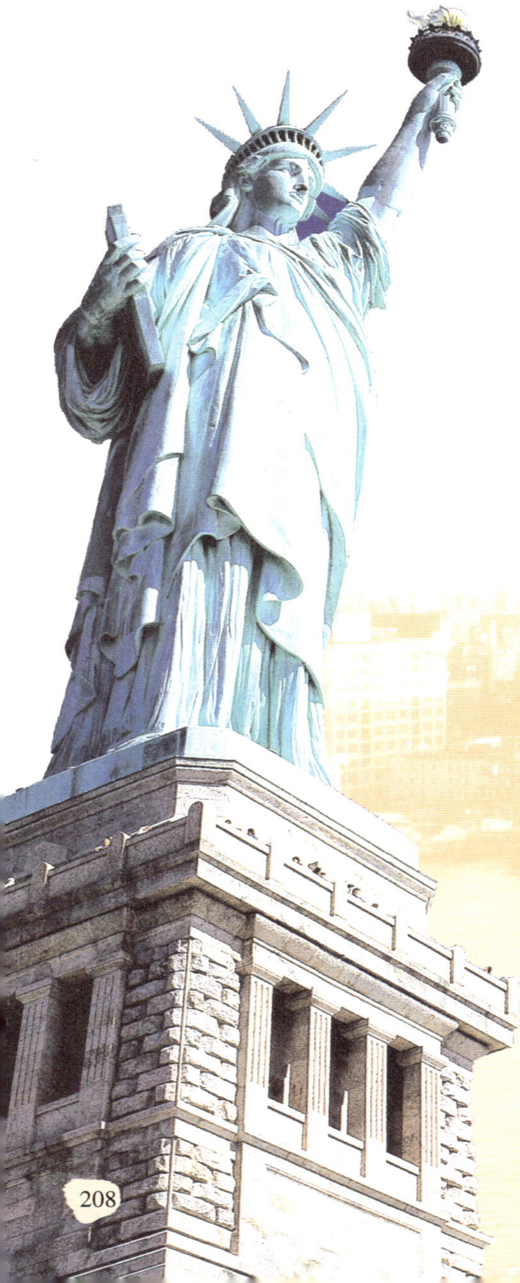

Daniel: Statue of Liberty is one of the symbols of the United States. It was a present from France to celebrate the 100th anniversary of the independence of the US.

Han Jia: Daniel, look over there. Is it Easter Island? It is so quick to come to South America.

场景 Scene 微缩复活节岛石像

大　牛：韩佳，你知道关于复活节岛的种种传说吗？

韩　佳：当然知道了。它是智利的一个小岛，岛上有一千多尊巨人石像，它们的由来至今还是个谜呢！

大　牛：传说是外星人建造的，因为他们的脸都是朝着天空看的，好像在等待什么似的④。有的说是岛上的土著人建造的，可是它们代表着什么，至今谁也说不清。

韩　佳：反正不管怎么说，能用一整块石头刻成10米高、50吨重的巨人石像也可以算得上是鬼斧神工了。⑤

大　牛：啊！你说是鬼神建造的？

韩　佳：我不是说真的是由鬼来建造的，我是用“鬼斧神工”来形容建造的技术太高超了，不是人力所能达到的。

大　牛：*我知道了，“鬼斧神工”是一个成语，形容建造技术高超。“鬼斧神工。”*

guǐ fǔ shén gōng

鬼斧神工

uncanny workmanship

韩　佳：大牛，你看那儿，石头上面怎么刻着那么多画儿啊？我们去看看！

大　牛：走！

Daniel: Han Jia, do you know the legends of Easter Island?

Han Jia: Of course I do. It is a small island of Chile. There are over 1000 giant stone statues on the island. It is still a mystery how they came here.

Daniel: Well, it is said a extraterrestrials built them, because they all look up to the sky. They seem to be waiting for something. Some say that they were built by the indigenes on the island. But nobody knows what they represent.

Han Jia: Anyway, it is a great craftsmanship to carve a whole stone into a giant stone statue which is 10-meter high and weighs 50 tons. In Chinese, we can say it was carved by "gui fu shen gong".

Daniel: Hey, you mean they were built by ghosts and immortals.

Han Jia: I didn't mean they were actually built by ghosts and immortals. I mean the craftsmanship is super. It is beyond people's capacity.

Daniel: I see. "Gui fu shen gong" is a Chinese idiom which means uncanny workmanship. "Gui fu shen gong".

Han Jia: Hey, Daniel, look over there. There are so many pictures carved on the stones. Let's go over and take a look.

Daniel: Let's go!

场景 Scene 那斯卡线画

大　牛：这就是秘鲁著名的那斯卡线画。韩佳，刚才你说了一个儿化韵哪！

韩　佳：这大牛的记性还真好，在我们以前的节目中教过儿化韵可以用来区分词性，又可以当动词，又可以当名词。如果加上儿化韵，“画儿”，那就一定是名词了。好了，大牛，该你给我讲讲这幅画儿的来历了。

大　牛：这个，这……我可说不清啊！

场景 Scene 巨石头像

韩　佳：哦，就是这个，够大的！这是个石头人头吧？

大　牛：没错，这就是在墨西哥发现的一个巨石头像。它有三米高，三十多吨重，是用整块的玄武石雕刻而成的。

韩　佳：这也算得上是一件艺术品了吧？可用它来做什么呢？

大　牛：这个，据我推测，它可能是某一个部落首领的头像。

Tā kěnéng shì mǒu gè bùluò shǒulǐng de tóuxiàng.

它 可能 是 某 个 部落 首领 的 头像。

It might be the sculpture of a certain tribal leader.

Daniel: This is the famous Nazca Lines in Peru. Han Jia, you just said an "erhuayun".

Han Jia: You do have good memory. We have learned "erhuayun" before. It can be used to differentiate the parts of speech. "Hua" can be used either as a verb or a noun. If we add "erhuayun", "huar" must be a noun. All right, Daniel, tell us about the history of the Nazca Lines.

Daniel: Well, well... I am not quite sure.

Han Jia: Well, here it is. It is really big. Is it a stone head?

Daniel: Right. This is a giant head sculpture discovered in Mexico. It is 3-meter high and weighs over 30 tons. It is made of a whole piece of basalt.

Han Jia: It can be regarded as an artwork. But what is it for?

Daniel: I guess it is a head sculpture of a certain clan chief.

场景 Scene 世界之窗内

韩　佳：瞧瞧我这身儿独特的印第安服装，肯定能吓大牛一跳，我先藏起来。

大　牛：观众朋友们，你们瞧我的这身新的打扮怎么样？一会儿准能吓韩佳一跳⑥，我先藏起来！

合：谁呀？

韩　佳：大牛！

大　牛：韩佳你也……

韩　佳：行了，别躲躲藏藏了，我们今天节目结束的时间就要到了。别忘了我们的口号：

合：学说中国话，朋友遍天下！

大　牛：跳舞去喽！

韩　佳：走喽！

Han Jia: Look at my unique Indian outfit. I will certainly astonish Daniel. Let me hide myself first.

Daniel: Audience friends, look, how about my new outfit? I will certainly astonish Han Jia. Let me hide myself first.

Together: Who is it?

Han Jia: Daniel.

Daniel: Han Jia,you ...

Han Jia: Don't hide yourself anymore. We are about to wrap up today's program. Don't forget our slogan.

Together: Learn Chinese and make friends everywhere.

Daniel: Let's go dancing.

Han Jia: Let's go.

世界之窗

生词 New Words and Expressions

1.	猜	（动）	cāi	to make a guess
2.	壮观	（形）	zhuàngguān	magnificent-looking
3.	独自	（副）	dúzì	alone
4.	不管	（连）	bùguǎn	no matter what
5.	鬼斧神工		guǐ fǔ shén gōng	uncanny workmanship
6.	发现	（动）	fāxiàn	to discover
7.	艺术品	（名）	yìshùpǐn	work of art
8.	推测	（动）	tuīcè	to conjesture
9.	部落	（名）	bùluò	tribe
10.	首领	（名）	shǒulǐng	chief

注释 Notes

1. 今天咱们是不是该去美洲了？

这是一个用“是不是”来提问的问句。如果提问的人对某事实或某情况已有比较肯定的估计，为了进一步得到证实，就可以用这种疑问句提问。“是不是”可以用在陈述句的谓语前，也可以用在句子的开头或最后。

This is a question with “是不是”. When a person who asks the question is quite sure of the answer, and wants to make further confirmation, he/she can use such a question form. “是不是” can be put before the predicate of the declarative sentence, or at the beginning or the end of the sentence.

例如：他是不是会说汉语？

是不是他会说汉语？

他会说汉语，是不是？

有时用“是不是”并不是为了得到证实，而是征求对方的同意，带有商量的口气。这个时候，“是不是”只能用在句子的谓语前或句子前，不能用在句子的后面。

Sometimes, this form of sentences is used to ask for agreement of the other side and is in a consultative tone. In this case, “是不是” can only be put before the predicate or at the beginning of the sentence. It can't be put at the end of the sentence.

例如：我们是不是给他打个电话？

是不是我们给他打个电话？

2. 但是看上去仍然很壮观。

"看上去"，插入语，从外表进行估计、打量。

"看上去", a parenthesis, means to make estimation and size up something from its outer appearance.

例如：他看上去年岁不小了，得有五十多岁。

3. 这也算得上是独出心裁了吧？

"算得上"，在这里的意思是"能算做……""可以认为是……"

"算得上" here means "can be counted as ..." or "can be considered as ..."

例如：林老师算得上是一个好老师。

4. 好像在等待什么似的。

"似的"，助词，用在名词、代词或动词后面，表示跟某种事物或情况相似。

"似的", an auxiliary word, is used after a noun, pronoun or verb, meaning similarity with certain things or situations.

例如：我进去，看他好像睡着了似的，所以不敢叫他。

5. 反正不管怎么说，能用一整块石头刻成10米高、50吨重的巨人石像也可以算得上是鬼斧神工了。

"不管……也（都）……"是一个条件复句，表示在任何条件或情况下结果都不会改变。

"不管……也（都）……" is a conditional complex sentence, and used to express the idea that the result will never change in any circumstances.

例如：他不管怎么忙，每天都（也）要锻炼一小时。

6. 一会儿准能吓韩佳一跳。

"准"，副词，相当于"一定"的意思。

"准", an adverb, means "must", or "to be bound to".

例如：你放心吧，星期天我准来。

替换练习 Substitution Drills

1. 这里有	白宫，	有	国会大厦，	还有	总统山。
	鲜花		草地		参天大树
	葡萄		山楂		脆甜的大梨
	理发店		饭馆		咖啡厅

2.	它	可能是某个	部落首领	的	头像。
	那		城市		标志
	她		文工团		演员
	这		公司		办公楼

会话 Conversations

完成下列对话　Complete the following dialogues
(如括号里有词语或提示，请按要求做　Use the words or phrases given in the brackets)

A: 你上哪儿去了？
B: 我去花店买花儿了。
A: 买花？现在花儿贵着呢！
B: ____________________，今天是我妈妈的生日。(不管……也……)

A: 这次考试他能考好吗？
B: 我想____________________。(准)
A: 你怎么这样说呢？
B: 他已经准备了两个星期了，我相信他一定能考好。

世界之窗

【第五集】

场景 Scene 世界之窗 非洲景区

大　牛：欢迎大家来到快乐非洲！

韩　佳：快乐非洲，你怎么连我们节目的名字都忘了？是《快乐中国》！

大　牛：没忘，没忘！今天，我们《快乐中国》带着大家来到了快乐的非洲。

韩　佳：没错，您看，热情的非洲朋友们正在欢迎大家呢！

场景 Scene 世界之窗 非洲景区

大　牛：哎呀！非洲的人们多热情啊！韩佳，你说，他们这么热情是不是因为非洲的天气太热了？

韩　佳：哪有这种解释呀？

Fēizhōurén duō rèqíng ā!

非洲人 多 热情 啊！

African people are so friendly!

Daniel: Welcome to Happy Africa.

Han Jia: Happy Africa? Did you forget the name of our show? It's *Happy China*!

Daniel: I didn't forget. Today, *Happy China* is taking you on a tour to the Happy Africa.

Han Jia: That's right. Look, the warm-hearted African friends are welcoming us.

Daniel: Wow, African people are so friendly! Han Jia, do you think that the reason for their hospitality has to do with Africa's hot temperature?

Han Jia: That's a strange idea ...

韩　佳：一到非洲我就会想到沙漠、骆驼，还有金字塔什么的。①

大　牛：韩佳，刚才你说的“什么的……”什么意思？

韩　佳：什么的，是我们生活中常用的口语词，表示话没有说完就省略掉了，和我们生活中常用的“等等”是一个意思。

大　牛：韩佳，刚才你说了你想看金字塔，想看就跟我来。

韩　佳：说来就来呀！②

场景 Scene　微缩金字塔　狮身人面像

大　牛：韩佳，这和你刚才说的景象差不多吧？

韩　佳：嗯！这是古埃及的狮身人面像，跟那边的金字塔一样，都是古埃及历史文化的见证。

大　牛：没错，那你知道这些是为谁建造的吗？

韩　佳：这是为埃及第四代法老哈夫拉建造的陵墓石像。这哈夫拉……大牛，你怎么一直在问我呀？你是知道的吧？

大　牛：你怎么才反应过来啊？③我当然知道了。这狮身人面像西方人称之为“Sphinx”，它是古希腊神话中一个人面怪物的名字。由于古埃及人把狮子作为力量的象征，所以才有了这种狮身人面的石像。

韩　佳：大牛刚才用“由于……所以……”说了一个表示因果关系的复句，跟我们以前学过的“因为……所以……”是一样的。我们可以说：“由于沙漠干燥缺水，所以植物很少。”

Yóuyú shāmò gānzào quē shuǐ, suǒyǐ zhíwù hěn shǎo.

由于 沙漠 干燥 缺 水，所以 植物 很 少。

Because the desert is so dry, very few plants grow there.

Han Jia: Once in Africa, I immediately think of desert, camels, pyramids, "shenmede ...".

Daniel: Han Jia, you just said "shenmede ...". What does it mean?

Han Jia: "Shenmede" is a spoken expression that means what's not said is omitted. It works the same as the expression "dengdeng...".

Daniel: Han Jia, you said you wanted to see pyramids? Then, follow me!

Han Jia: Here we come!

Daniel: Han Jia, is this what you had in mind?

Han Jia: Yes. The Sphinx of Egypt, just like those pyramids, is a witness of Egypt's history and culture.

Daniel: That's right. Then do you know who they were built for?

Han Jia: It's a stone sculpture built for Egypt's fourth pharaoh, Khafre. Pharoah Khafre ... Why are you asking me all this, Daniel? You already know it, don't you?

Daniel: You just realized that? Of course, I know it. The lion with a man's head is called Sphinx. It's the name of a man-faced monster in Greek mythology. Because the ancient Egyptians saw lions as the sign of power, so they constructed this image of the Sphinx.

Han Jia: Daniel, you just used "youyu ... suoyi ..." to say a cause-effect compound sentence. It's the same as "yinwei ... suoyi ..." as we learned before. We can say, "youyu" the desert is so dry and short of water, "suoyi" very few plants can grow there.

场景 Scene 非洲丛林

大　牛：这是什么呀？韩佳，你把我领到哪儿了？

韩　佳：还好意思问我，不是说你带我游非洲吗？怎么现在反过来问我呢？

大　牛：这应该是非洲丛林了吧？

韩　佳：你呀，还是听我说吧！④非洲不但有一望无际的沙漠，而且还有热带原始丛林。这里有各种各样的动物，它们嬉戏玩耍，过着自由自在的生活，真可以说这里是动物们的天堂。

大　牛：韩佳，你怎么像是在主持动物世界似的？不过我还听出来了，你用了一个"不但……而且……"。

韩　佳：没错，"不但……而且……"是表示递进关系的。我们还可以说："热带丛林不但是植物的王国，而且是动物的世界。"

Zhèli búdàn shì zhíwù wángguó, érqiě shì dòngwù shìjiè.

这里不但是植物王国，而且是动物世界。

This is not only a plant kingdom, it's also an animal world.

Daniel: What is this? Where have you taken me?

Han Jia: You're asking me? Didn't you say that you were guiding the African tour?

Daniel: This ought to be an African jungle.

Han Jia: Never mind, just listen to me. Besides boundless deserts, Africa also has primitive tropical forests. All kinds of animals live and play around here. They lead happy and free lives here. We can call it animals' paradise.

Daniel: Han Jia, it sounds like you're hosting Animal World. But I noticed that you used "budan ... erqie ...".

Han Jia: Right. "Budan ... erqie ..." expresses a progressive relationship. For example, tropical forests is not only a plant kingdom, but an animal world.

世界之窗

场景 Scene　动物群雕

大　牛：韩佳，快来看！这里有那么多牛在跑啊，足有上万头呢！⑤

韩　佳：什么牛啊，这是非洲角马！你看，它们往一个地方跑。你知道它们是在做什么吗？

大　牛：当然知道了，它们在搬家呢！

韩　佳：差不多，这叫“迁徙”。“迁徙”就是“迁移，离开原来居住的地方”。

大　牛：英文我们可以说“migrate”。

韩　佳：对，我想它们肯定是找到了一个更好的地方。在那里有更多的草地供它们无忧无虑地生活⑥，所以它们才会迁徙的。我说得没错吧？大牛，这大牛又跑到哪儿去了？大牛！

Daniel: Look, Han Jia ... there are so many oxen running! There got to be ten thousand of them.

Han Jia: Oxen? These are African gnus. They're all running to the same direction. Do you know what they're doing?

Daniel: Of course, they're moving!

Han Jia: Close enough. It's called "qianxi". It means to migrate, to leave the old place.

Daniel: In English, we could say "migrate".

Han Jia: Yes. I think they must have found a better place. There, they would have more grass and lead a carefree life. That's why they would migrate. Am I right, Daniel? Daniel? Where did he go? Daniel?

场景 Scene 毛利民居

韩　佳：明明看见大牛进去了，怎么一下子就不见了呀？⑦那边有个人，我去问问他。你好，请问看见大牛了吗？这不会就是传说中的食人部落吧？大牛，快出来，有危险！

场景 Scene 毛利民居

韩　佳：大牛！

大　牛：韩佳，你不用害怕，他们这是在欢迎你呢！这里是大洋洲新西兰毛利民居，正准备和他们一起跳舞狂欢呢！

韩　佳：你打扮成这个样子，我都认不出来了，刚才可把我给吓坏了。你要狂欢，也得跟我们的观众朋友们先告个别嘛！

大　牛：对了，别忘了我们的口号：

合：学说中国话，朋友遍天下！

Han Jia: I just saw Daniel go inside ... How come he disappeared? I'll go and ask that man over there. Hello, have you seen Daniel? I hope this is not the legendary tribe of cannibals! Come out, Daniel! It's dangerous!

Han Jia: Daniel!

Daniel: Relax, Han Jia ... They're just greeting you. This is the civilian residence of New Zealand's Maoris. I'm getting ready to sing and dance with them.

Han Jia: I couldn't even recognize you in this costume. I was really horrified. Before you get carried away by wild pleasure, say goodbye to everyone first.

Daniel: Right. Don't forget our slogan:

Together: Learn Chinese and make friends everywhere!

生词 New Words and Expressions

1.	解释	（动）	jiěshì	to explain
2.	反应	（动）	fǎnyìng	to react
3.	沙漠	（名）	shāmò	desert
4.	干燥	（形）	gānzào	dry
5.	植物	（名）	zhíwù	plant
6.	动物	（名）	dòngwù	animal
7.	自由自在		zìyóu zìzài	leisurely and carefree
8.	王国	（名）	wángguó	kingdom
9.	供	（动）	gōng	to supply
10.	无忧无虑		wú yōu wú lǜ	carefree

注释 Notes

1. 一到非洲我就会想到沙漠、骆驼，还有金字塔什么的。

"什么的"用在一个成分或几个并列成分后，相当于"等等"，常用于口语。

"什么的" used after an element or several coordinate elements in a sentence, is equivalent to "等等"("and so on" in English). It is often used in spoken Chinese.

例如：每天中午他就喜欢吃饺子、面条什么的，不喜欢吃米饭。

2. 说来就来呀！

"说……就……"这一结构说明动作或事情发生很快，很突然。

The structure "说……就……" indicates that something happens instantly or suddenly.

例如：他说走就走，多一会儿都不想待。

3. 你怎么才反应过来啊？

"过来"用在动词后表示回到正常的状态。

"过来" used after a verb indicates the return to normal state.

例如：今天早上他七点半才醒过来。

4. 你呀，还是听我说吧！

"还是"，副词，在这里表示经过比较、考虑后作出的选择。

"还是"，an adverb, indicates one's decision-making after deliberation and comparison.

例如：我看还是星期天去吧，星期天大家都有时间。

5．这里有那么多牛在跑啊，足有上万头呢！

"上"，动词，在这里表示达到一定的数量，常带数量宾语。

"上"，a verb, indicates a certain amount, often followed by an object of numerals.

例如：这个景点不错，每天都有上千人来参观。

6．在那里有更多的草地供它们无忧无虑地生活。

"地"，结构助词，状语的书写标志，表示它前边的词或词组是状语。

"地"，a structural auxiliary word in written Chinese, indicates that words or phrases before it function as an adverbial.

例如：经过两个小时的努力，他们胜利地爬上了山顶。

7．明明看见大牛进去了，怎么一下子就不见了呀？

"明明"，副词，表示显然是这样，在用"明明"的句子后，常有反问或表示转折的句子。

"明明", an adverb, means "obviously". Rhetorical or transitional sentences often follow the sentence with this expression.

例如：他明明是这样说的，现在为什么不承认了呢？

替换练习 Substitution Drills

1. 非洲人	多	热情	啊！
这里的湖水		清澈	
北京的雪景		美	
这里的物产		丰富	

2. 由于	沙漠干燥缺水，	所以	植物很少。
	他每天锻炼		身体很好
	她学习刻苦		成绩优异
	马路上大雪堆积		交通堵塞

3. 这里	不但	是植物王国，	而且	是动物世界。
那里		物产丰富		景色宜人
她		是好学生		是优秀运动员
这件衣服		样式好看		价格合理

会话 Conversations

完成下列对话　Complete the following dialogues
（如括号里有词语或提示，请按要求做　Use the words or phrases given in the brackets）

A: 你上哪儿去了？
B: 看见了。我＿＿＿＿＿＿，怎么一下子就不见了？（明明）
A: 会不会进去了？
B: 我去看一下儿。

A: 参观这个景点的人每天都这么多吗？
B: 每天都这么多。
A: 这一天得有多少人？
B: ＿＿＿＿＿＿。（上）

畅游深圳 温馨提示

城市风情

深圳是一个新兴城市，独有的特区文化现象表现为高效率和快节奏。

最宜人的季节

四季皆宜，8月、9月为最佳，年平均温度22.3°C。

最舒适的着装

春夏休闲装

必游景点

民俗文化村	欢乐谷	世界之窗	蛇口水上世界
西丽湖	地王大厦	明思克航母	深圳野生动物园
香蜜湖	仙湖植物园	青青世界	小梅沙海滨旅游区

风味特产／地方美食

南山荔枝	坪山金龟橘	西丽芒果	石岩沙梨
沙井鲜蚝	西乡基围虾	南澳鲍鱼	福永乌头鱼
龙岗三黄鸡	松岗腊鸭	公明烧鹅	

另有：土产药材。

与外交通

航空：深圳宝安机场距市中心32公里，现除了与直辖市及各省会城市（除拉萨）通航外，还与北海、常德、常州、大连、丹东、广元、宜宾、张家界、湛江等众多城市通航。

铁路：深圳处京九与广九铁路交汇处，与九龙、广州之间每日有数十班列车往返，与北京、郑州、合肥、武昌、长沙等均有直通列车。

另有：便捷的公路和水运交通。

特别提示

每年6月28日—7月8日举行荔枝节，为深圳的市节。

（京）新登字 157 号

图书在版编目（CIP）数据

快乐中国——学汉语：深圳篇 /《快乐中国——学汉语》栏目组编.
—北京：北京语言大学出版社，2006
ISBN 7-5619-1569-1

Ⅰ. 快…
Ⅱ. 快…
Ⅲ. 汉语-视听教学-对外汉语教学-教材
Ⅳ. H195.4

中国版本图书馆 CIP 数据核字（2006）第 005037 号

书　　名：快乐中国——学汉语：深圳篇
责任编辑：王亚莉　武思敏
封面设计：张志伟　李关栋
责任印制：汪学发

出版发行：北京语言大学出版社
社　　址：北京市海淀区学院路 15 号　邮政编码：100083
网　　址：http://www.blcup.com
电　　话：发行部　82303650 / 3591 / 3651
编辑部　82303647
读者服务部　82303653 / 3908
印　　刷：北京中科印刷有限公司
经　　销：全国新华书店

版　　次：2006 年 5 月第 1 版　2006 年 5 月第 1 次印刷
开　　本：710 毫米×980 毫米　1/16　**印张**：15.5
字　　数：225 千字　**印数**：1-4000 册
书　　号：ISBN 7-5619-1569-1 / H·05220
定　　价：79.00 元

凡有印装质量问题，本社负责调换。电话：82303590